Magical Wonderland ™

The Needlecraft Shop®

www.NeedlecraftShop.com

PRODUCT DEVELOPMENT DIRECTOR	Andy Ashley
PUBLISHING SERVICES DIRECTOR	Ange Van Arman
PLASTIC CANVAS DESIGN MANAGER	Fran Rohus
PRODUCT DEVELOPMENT STAFF	Mickie Akins
	Darla Hassell
	Sandra Miller Maxfield
	Alice Vaughan
	Ann White
SENIOR EDITOR	Judy Crow
EDITOR	Kris Kirst
ASSOCIATE EDITORS	Jeanne Austin
	Shirley Brown
	Jaimie Davenport
	Shirley Patrick
COLOR SPECIALIST/SUPERVISOR	Betty Holmes
GRAPHIC DESIGNER	Glenda Chamberlain
PHOTOGRAPHY MANAGER	Scott Campbell
PHOTOGRAPHERS	Keith Godfrey
	Tammy Coquat-Payne
	Andy J. Burnfield
PHOTO STYLIST	Martha Coquat
CUSTOMER SERVICE	1-800-449-0440
PATTERN SERVICES	(903) 636-5140 or write to: The Needlecraft Shop Plastic Canvas Editors (address below)
CHIEF EXECUTIVE OFFICER	John Robinson
MARKETING DIRECTOR	Scott Moss

Credits

Sincerest thanks to all the designers, manufacturers and other professionals whose dedication has made this book possible.

Library of Congress Cataloging-in-Publication Data
ISBN: 1-57367-114-2
First Printing: 2000
Library of Congress Catalog Card Number: 00-91849
Published and Distributed by
The Needlecraft Shop, LLC, Big Sandy, Texas 75755
Printed in the United States of America.

Ever wish

you could whisk yourself away to a magical land? A place that children laugh and dance and so do all the grown-up people? A place you can stitch plastic canvas needlepoint to your hearts content?

Welcome to *Magical Wonderland*! This is not just another plastic canvas book, it's a journey through a wonderland of wintry delights, a place we can laugh and dance and enjoy plastic canvas till our hearts are full!

As you start your journey you will meet our host, the frosty snow people at the beginning of each chapter. They will help guide you through the wintry trail where you will meet new Christmas friends, sparkling angels and playful snowbirds. Your heart will be warmed with the remembrance of Christmas past and the faint smell of gingerbread you're sure you just smelled.

As your adventures continue, you may begin to notice a small giggle escaping your lips and a little tap in your fingertips, ready for stitching. No problem! Our frosty host will patiently wait for you, for however long you need to stitch up some Christmas merriment of your very own. When you're finished, they'll still be there waiting for you.

Grab your stocking cap, mittens and plastic canvas supplies and dive into a fantasyland of plastic canvas Christmas fun, *Magical Wonderland*!

Fran

Fran Rohus

table of contents

holy beginnings

snow friends

country charm

yuletide traditions

glimmer & glow

angel gathering

We begin our magical adventure in the true spirit of Christmas, as our nativity snow couple guide us through the snowy lanes of our inspired beginnings, reminding us of the peaceful and jubilant meaning of the holiday.

designed by
Christine A. Hendricks

snowman *manger*

skill level & size

Average skill level. 11½" x 18" [29.2cm x 45.7cm].

materials

- One 12" x 18" [30.5cm x 45.7cm] or larger sheet of 7-count plastic canvas
- Fine metallic braid or metallic thread; for amount see Color Key.
- Six-strand embroidery floss; for amount see Color Key.
- Worsted-weight or plastic canvas yarn; for amounts see Color Key.

cutting instructions

For Snowman Manger, cut one 76 x 118 holes.

stitching instructions

1: Using colors and stitches indicated, work picture according to graph; fill in uncoded areas using white and Continental Stitch. With holly, Overcast edges.

2: Using braid or thread, camel yarn and three strands floss in colors and embroidery stitches indicated, embroider detail as indicated on graph.

3: Hang or display as desired. ☀

COLOR KEY: Snowman Manger

Metallic braid or thread		Kreinik Tapestry™	AMOUNT
Gold		#002	3 yds. [2.7m]

Embroidery floss		DMC®	AMOUNT
Black		#310	16 yds. [14.6m]

Worsted-weight	Nylon Plus™	Need-loft®	YARN AMOUNT
White	#01	#41	3 oz. [85.1m]
Holly	#31	#27	20 yds. [18.3m]
Yellow	#26	#57	17 yds. [15.5m]
Flesh Tone	–	#56	12 yds. [11m]
Watermelon	#54	#55	11 yds. [10.1m]
Baby Green	#28	–	8 yds. [7.3m]
Lemon	#25	#20	8 yds. [7.3m]
Sail Blue	#04	#35	7 yds. [6.4m]
Maple	#35	#13	5 yds. [4.6m]
Pink	#11	#07	3 yds. [2.7m]
Tangerine	#15	#11	3 yds. [2.7m]
Black	#02	#00	2 yds. [1.8m]
Gray	#23	#38	2 yds. [1.8m]
Pumpkin	#50	#12	2 yds. [1.8m]
Royal Dark	#07	#48	2 yds. [1.8m]
Silver	–	#37	2 yds. [1.8m]
Camel	#34	#43	1 yd. [0.9m]

STITCH KEY:

- — Backstitch/Straight
- ● French Knot

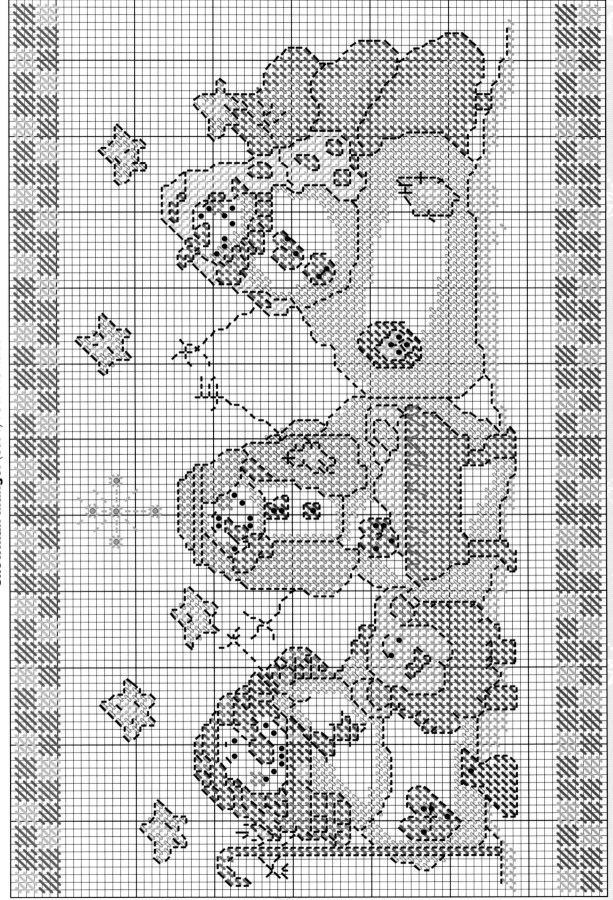

Snowman Manger (cut 1) 76 x 118 holes

holy beginnings

beribboned treasures

designed by
Ruby Thacker

skill level & sizes

Average skill level. Purple Frame is 5½" x 7⅜" [14cm x 18.7cm] with a 2½" x 4¼" [6.4cm x 10.8cm] photo window; Purple Ornament is 1½" x 4" [3.8cm x 10.2cm]; Green Frame is 5" x 6¾" [12.7cm x 17.1cm] with a 2¾" x 4½" [7cm x 11.4cm] photo window; Green Ornament is 2⅛" x 2½" [5.4cm x 6.4cm]; Burgundy Frame is 5⅛" square [13cm] with a 3" square [7.6cm] photo window; Burgundy Ornament is 4½" x 4½" [11.4cm x 11.4cm]. Measurements do not include tassels.

materials for one set

- One sheet of 7-count plastic canvas
- One metallic gold 3" [7.6cm] tassel
- 1 yd. [0.9m] of fine metallic braid or metallic thread
- 2 yds. [1.8m] gold 4mm strung pearls (for Purple Set)
- Four gold ¾" [19mm] oval cabochon stones (for Purple Set)
- Six red satin 1½" [3.8cm] poinsettias (for Green Set)
- Miniature artificial pinecones with berries and greenery (for Green Set)
- Two 1" [2.5cm] oval amber cabochon stones (for Burgundy Set)
- Monofilament fishing line
- Craft glue or glue gun
- ⅛" [3mm] satin ribbon or worsted-weight yarn; for amounts see individual Color Keys on pages 12 and 13.

purple set
cutting instructions

A: For Frame front and backing, cut one according to graph for front and one 37 x 49 holes for backing (no backing graph).

B: For Frame stand, cut one according to graph.

C: For Ornament sides, cut four according to graph.

stitching instructions

NOTE: Backing A and B pieces are not worked.

1: Using colors and stitches indicated, work front A and C pieces according to graphs; with purple, Overcast cutout edges of front A.

2: Whipstitch A and B pieces together according to Frame Assembly Diagram.

3: Glue strung pearls around Frame front as indicated on A graph and as shown in photo, trimming as needed to fit.

NOTE: Cut one 12" [30.5cm] length of braid or thread.

4: For ornament, Whipstitch and assemble C pieces, tassel and braid as shown and according to Ornament Assembly Diagram. Glue one gold cabochon to each side of Ornament.

green set
cutting instructions

A: For Frame front and backing, cut one according to graph for front and one 33 x 45 holes for backing (no backing graph).

B: For Frame stand, cut one according to Purple Set B graph.

C: For Ornament sides, cut four according to graph.

stitching instructions

NOTE: Backing A and B pieces are not worked.

1: Using colors and stitches indicated, work front A and C pieces according to graphs; with gold, Overcast cutout edges of front A.

2: Substituting gold for purple, Whipstitch A and B pieces together according to Frame Assembly Diagram.

3: Glue pinecones, leaves, berries and two poinsettias to Frame as shown in photo.

NOTE: Cut one 12" [30.5cm] length of braid or thread.

4: For Ornament, Whipstitch and assemble C pieces, tassel and braid according to Ornament Assembly Diagram. Glue one remaining poinsettia to each side of Ornament.

burgundy set
cutting instructions

A: For Frame front and backing, cut one according to graph for front and one 34 x 34 holes for backing (no backing graph).

B: For Frame stand, cut one according to Purple Set B graph.

C: For Ornament pieces, cut two according to graph.

stitching instructions

NOTE: Backing A and B pieces are not worked.

1: Using colors and stitches indicated, work front A and C pieces according to graphs; with gold, Overcast cutout edges of front A.

2: Substituting gold for purple, Whipstitch A and B pieces together according to Frame Assembly Diagram.

NOTE: Cut one 12" [30.5cm] length of braid or thread.

3: For Ornament, with gold, Whipstitch C pieces wrong sides together. Fold braid or thread in half and thread cut ends through s hole on Ornament as indicated on graph. Pull ends to even, tie into a knot and trim close to knot. Glue one amber stone to each side of Ornament and tassel to bottom (see photo). ✳

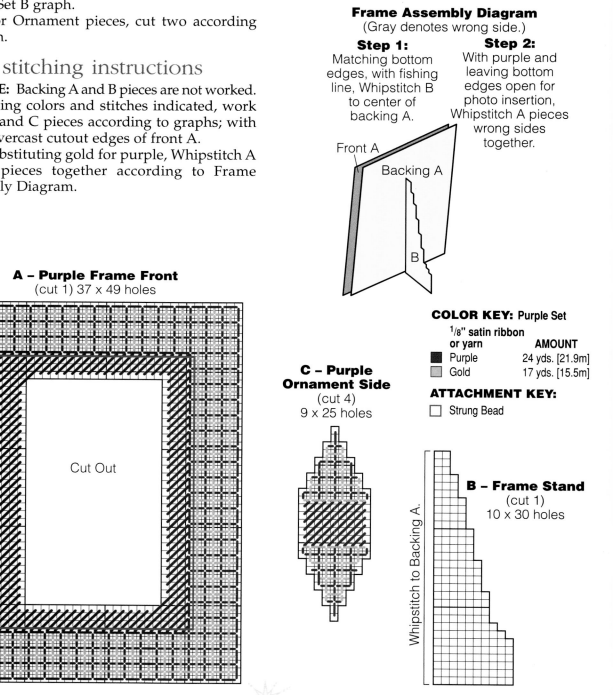

Frame Assembly Diagram
(Gray denotes wrong side.)

Step 1:
Matching bottom edges, with fishing line, Whipstitch B to center of backing A.

Step 2:
With purple and leaving bottom edges open for photo insertion, Whipstitch A pieces wrong sides together.

Front A

Backing A

B

A – Purple Frame Front
(cut 1) 37 x 49 holes

Cut Out

C – Purple Ornament Side
(cut 4)
9 x 25 holes

COLOR KEY: Purple Set

1/8" satin ribbon or yarn	AMOUNT
■ Purple	24 yds. [21.9m]
▨ Gold	17 yds. [15.5m]

ATTACHMENT KEY:
☐ Strung Bead

B – Frame Stand
(cut 1)
10 x 30 holes

Whipstitch to Backing A.

holy beginnings

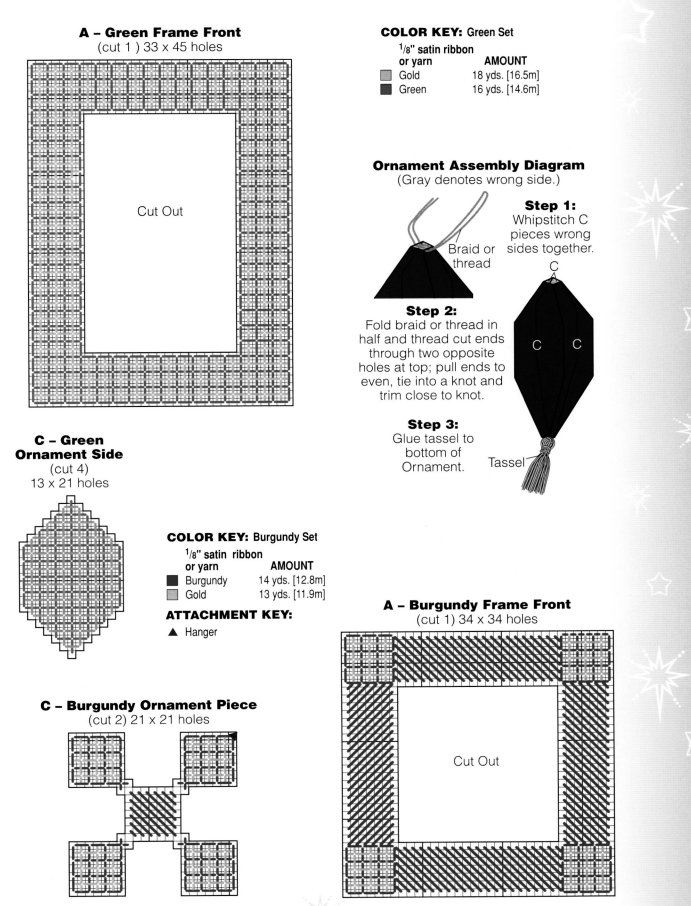

A – Green Frame Front
(cut 1) 33 x 45 holes

Cut Out

COLOR KEY: Green Set
1/8" satin ribbon
or yarn   AMOUNT
Gold   18 yds. [16.5m]
Green   16 yds. [14.6m]

Ornament Assembly Diagram
(Gray denotes wrong side.)

Braid or thread

Step 1:
Whipstitch C pieces wrong sides together.

C

Step 2:
Fold braid or thread in half and thread cut ends through two opposite holes at top; pull ends to even, tie into a knot and trim close to knot.

C   C

Step 3:
Glue tassel to bottom of Ornament.

Tassel

C – Green Ornament Side
(cut 4)
13 x 21 holes

COLOR KEY: Burgundy Set
1/8" satin ribbon
or yarn   AMOUNT
Burgundy   14 yds. [12.8m]
Gold   13 yds. [11.9m]

ATTACHMENT KEY:
▲ Hanger

C – Burgundy Ornament Piece
(cut 2) 21 x 21 holes

A – Burgundy Frame Front
(cut 1) 34 x 34 holes

Cut Out

holy beginnings

designed by
Kristine
Loffredo

we three kings

skill level & size

Average skill level. 9" x 27" [22.9cm x 68.6cm], not including raffia.

materials

- Two sheets of 7-count plastic canvas
- One package of natural raffia
- Craft glue or glue gun
- Worsted-weight or plastic canvas yarn; for amounts see Color Key.

cutting instructions

A: For first king, cut one according to graph.
B: For first king's mustache, cut one according to graph.

A – First King
(cut 1) 39 x 70 holes

C – First King's Gems
(cut 2)
5 x 5 holes

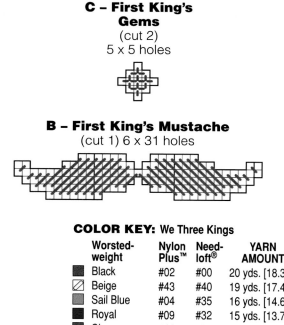

B – First King's Mustache
(cut 1) 6 x 31 holes

STITCH KEY:
— Backstitch/Straight
× Cross Stitch

COLOR KEY: We Three Kings

Worsted-weight	Nylon Plus™	Need-loft®	YARN AMOUNT
Black	#02	#00	20 yds. [18.3m]
Beige	#43	#40	19 yds. [17.4m]
Sail Blue	#04	#35	16 yds. [14.6m]
Royal	#09	#32	15 yds. [13.7m]
Cinnamon	#44	#14	11 yds. [10.1m]
Bright Purple	–	#64	7 yds. [6.4m]
Brown	#36	#15	6 yds. [5.5m]
Xmas Red	#19	#02	6 yds. [5.5m]
Pewter	#40	–	4 yds. [3.7m]
Gold	#27	#17	3 yds. [2.7m]
Burgundy	#13	#03	2 yds. [2.7m]
Purple	#21	#46	2 yds. [1.8m]
Xmas Green	#58	#28	2 yds. [1.8m]
Lavender	#12	#05	1 yd. [0.9m]
Turquoise	#03	#54	½ yd. [0.5m]
Royal Dark	#07	#48	¼ yd. [0.2m]

holy beginnings

C: For first king's gems, cut two according to graph.

D: For second king, cut one according to graph.

E: For second king's mustache, cut one according to graph.

F: For second king's gems #1 and #2, cut one each according to graphs.

G: For third king, cut one according to graph.

H: For third king's mustache, cut one according to graph.

I: For third king's gems #1–#3, cut number indicated according to graphs.

stitching instructions

1: Using colors and stitches indicated, work A–F#1 and G–I pieces according to graphs; with Xmas green for Second King's gem #2, royal for Second King and with matching colors, Overcast edges of pieces.

2: Using gold (Separate into individual plies, if desired.) and embroidery stitches indicated, embroider detail on A as indicated on graph.

3: To form banner, glue A, D and G together as shown in photo; glue corresponding mustaches and gems to right side of each king as shown.

NOTE: Remove eight strands of raffia from package.

4: Holding all strands together, tie into a knot about 12" [30.5cm] from one end. Glue knot to wrong side of first king. Fan out strands behind banner. ✷

E – Second King's Mustache
(cut 1) 5 x 21 holes

F – Second King's Gem #1
(cut 1)
3 x 3 holes

F – Second King's Gem #2
(cut 1)
3 x 3 holes

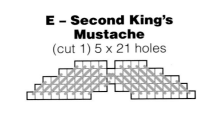

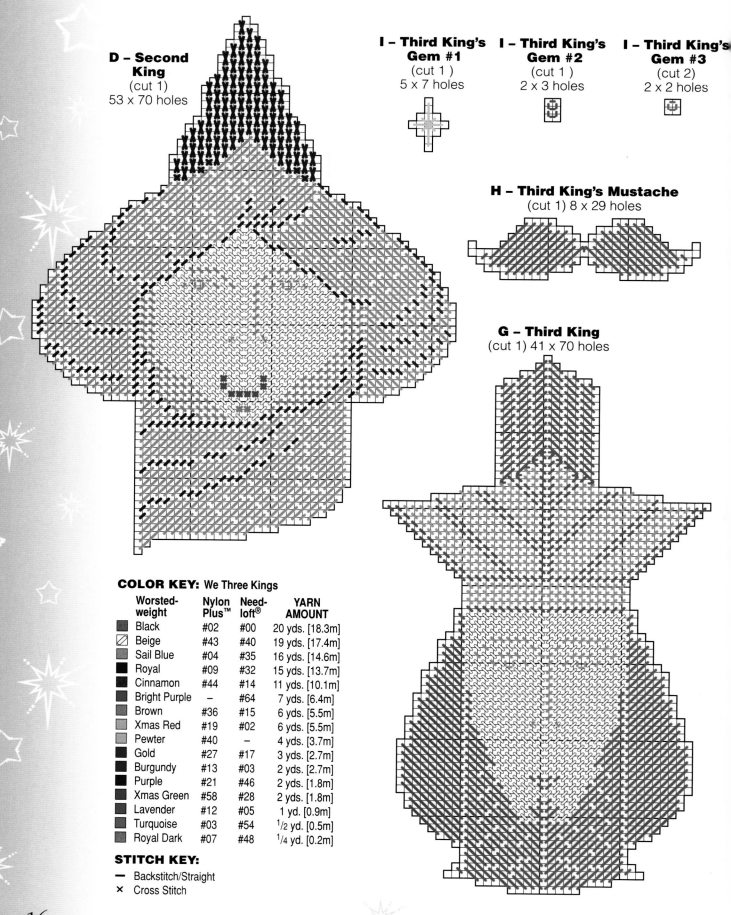

D – Second King
(cut 1)
53 x 70 holes

I – Third King's Gem #1
(cut 1)
5 x 7 holes

I – Third King's Gem #2
(cut 1)
2 x 3 holes

I – Third King's Gem #3
(cut 2)
2 x 2 holes

H – Third King's Mustache
(cut 1) 8 x 29 holes

G – Third King
(cut 1) 41 x 70 holes

COLOR KEY: We Three Kings

	Worsted-weight	Nylon Plus™	Need-loft®	YARN AMOUNT
	Black	#02	#00	20 yds. [18.3m]
	Beige	#43	#40	19 yds. [17.4m]
	Sail Blue	#04	#35	16 yds. [14.6m]
	Royal	#09	#32	15 yds. [13.7m]
	Cinnamon	#44	#14	11 yds. [10.1m]
	Bright Purple	–	#64	7 yds. [6.4m]
	Brown	#36	#15	6 yds. [5.5m]
	Xmas Red	#19	#02	6 yds. [5.5m]
	Pewter	#40	–	4 yds. [3.7m]
	Gold	#27	#17	3 yds. [2.7m]
	Burgundy	#13	#03	2 yds. [2.7m]
	Purple	#21	#46	2 yds. [1.8m]
	Xmas Green	#58	#28	2 yds. [1.8m]
	Lavender	#12	#05	1 yd. [0.9m]
	Turquoise	#03	#54	1/2 yd. [0.5m]
	Royal Dark	#07	#48	1/4 yd. [0.2m]

STITCH KEY:

— Backstitch/Straight
× Cross Stitch

holy beginnings

deluxe
gift boxes

designed by
Ruby Thacker

skill level & sizes

Average skill level. Large Box is 10½" across x 4¾" tall [26.7cm x 12.1cm]; Small Box is 5½" across x 4⅞" tall [14cm x 12.4cm].

materials

- Six Uniek, Inc. 5" [12.7cm] hexagon shapes
- Two sheets of forest green and three sheets of clear 7-count plastic canvas

holy beginnings

- 1½ yds. [1.4m] of forest green/burgundy ³⁄₁₆"
  [4.5mm] twisted cord
- Six gold ⅝" [16mm] shank buttons of choice
  (for Large Box)
- Three gold ⅝" [16mm] shank heart buttons
  (for Small Box)
- Six burgundy and three forest green 4"
  [10.2cm] tassels
- Sewing needle and thread to match tassels
- Craft glue or glue gun
- Metallic cord; for amount see Color Key.
- Worsted-weight or plastic canvas yarn; for
  amounts see Color Key.

large box
cutting instructions

A: For lid center, use one hexagon shape.

B: For lid outer pieces #1 and #2, cut one each from each of three hexagon shapes according to graphs.

C: For lid side pieces, cut six from forest green 13 x 35 holes (no graph).

D: For lid lining, cut one according to graph.

E: For box sides, cut six from clear 30 x 33 holes (no graph).

F: For box bottom, cut one according to graph.

stitching instructions

NOTE: D and F pieces are not worked.

1: Using colors and stitches indicated, work A and B pieces according to graphs; using forest and Continental Stitch, work C and E pieces.

2: Whipstitch pieces together as indicated on graph and according to Large Box Assembly Diagram.

NOTE: Cut a 1-yd. [0.9m] length of twisted cord.

3: Attach cord, one button and one burgundy tassel to lid according to Large Box Tassel Attachment Diagram.

small box
cutting instructions

A: For lid top, use one hexagon shape (no graph).

B: For lid sides, cut six from clear 7 x 18 holes (no graph).

C: For box sides, cut six from clear 16 x 30 holes (no graph).

D: For box bottom, cut away outer row of holes from remaining hexagon shape (no graph).

**Large Box Tassel
Attachment Diagram**
(Pieces are shown in different
colors for contrast.)

Step 1:
Drape cord around lid, using sewing needle and thread to sew cord to lid at each corner seam as you work.

Lid   Cord

(enlarged view)

Step 2:
Slip hanging loop of tassel over button shank; with matching thread, tack button to corner of lid.

Button
Shank

Tassel

A – Large Box Lid Center
(use one hexagon shape)

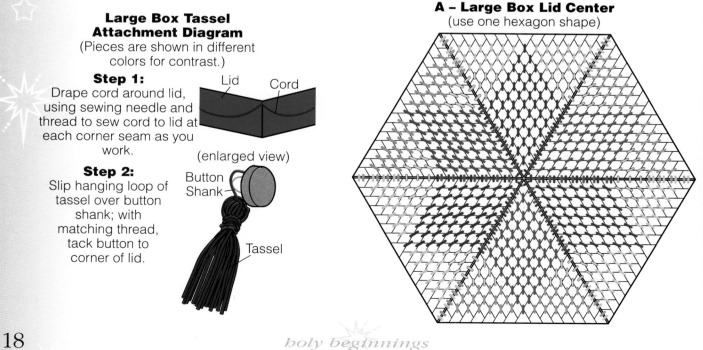

holy beginnings

stitching instructions

NOTE: D is not worked.

1: Using colors and stitches indicated, work A according to Large Box A graph; using burgundy yarn and Continental Stitch, work B and C pieces.

2: With burgundy yarn, Whipstitch pieces together according to Small Box Assembly Diagram.

3: Assemble remaining twisted cord, heart buttons and forest green tassels according to Small Box Tassel Attachment Diagram. ✳

Large Box Assembly Diagram
(Pieces are shown in different colors for contrast; gray denotes wrong side.)

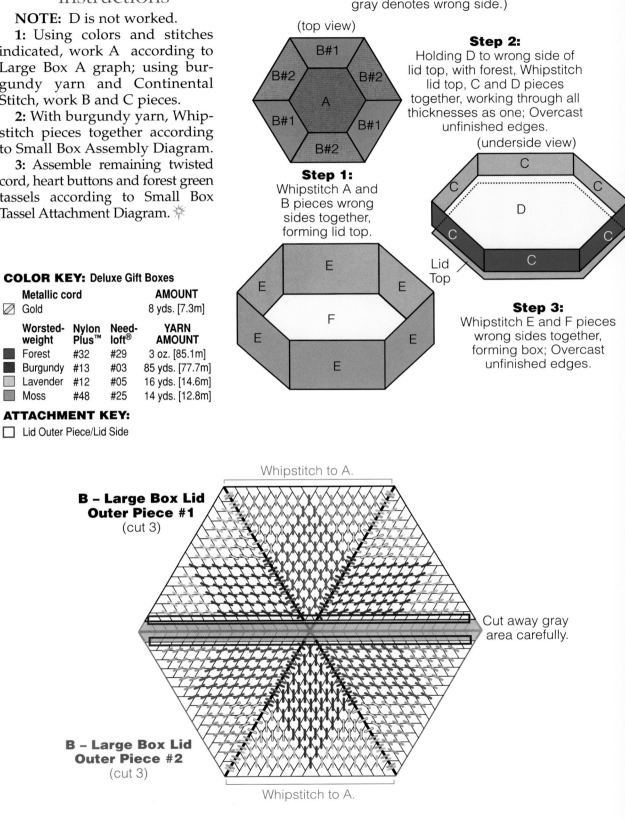

(top view)

Step 1:
Whipstitch A and B pieces wrong sides together, forming lid top.

Step 2:
Holding D to wrong side of lid top, with forest, Whipstitch lid top, C and D pieces together, working through all thicknesses as one; Overcast unfinished edges.

(underside view)

Lid Top

Step 3:
Whipstitch E and F pieces wrong sides together, forming box; Overcast unfinished edges.

COLOR KEY: Deluxe Gift Boxes

	Metallic cord			AMOUNT
▨	Gold			8 yds. [7.3m]

	Worsted-weight	Nylon Plus™	Need-loft®	YARN AMOUNT
■	Forest	#32	#29	3 oz. [85.1m]
■	Burgundy	#13	#03	85 yds. [77.7m]
■	Lavender	#12	#05	16 yds. [14.6m]
■	Moss	#48	#25	14 yds. [12.8m]

ATTACHMENT KEY:

☐ Lid Outer Piece/Lid Side

Whipstitch to A.

B – Large Box Lid Outer Piece #1
(cut 3)

Cut away gray area carefully.

B – Large Box Lid Outer Piece #2
(cut 3)

Whipstitch to A.

Small Box Tassel Attachment Diagram

(Pieces are shown in different colors for contrast; gray denotes wrong side.)

Step 1:
Slide cord through button shanks, spacing buttons 6" [15.2cm] apart.

Step 2:
With matching thread, tack one tassel to back of each button.

Step 3:
Alternating sides, tack one button to center of each lid side; glue ends of cord to box to secure.

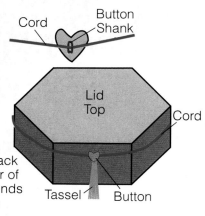

Small Box Assembly Diagram

(Pieces are shown in different colors for contrast; gray denotes wrong side.)

Step 1:
Whipstitch A and B pieces wrong sides together, forming lid.

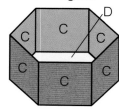

Step 2:
Whipstitch C and D pieces wrong sides together, forming box.

D – Large Box Lid Lining
(cut 1 from forest green) 60 x 69 holes

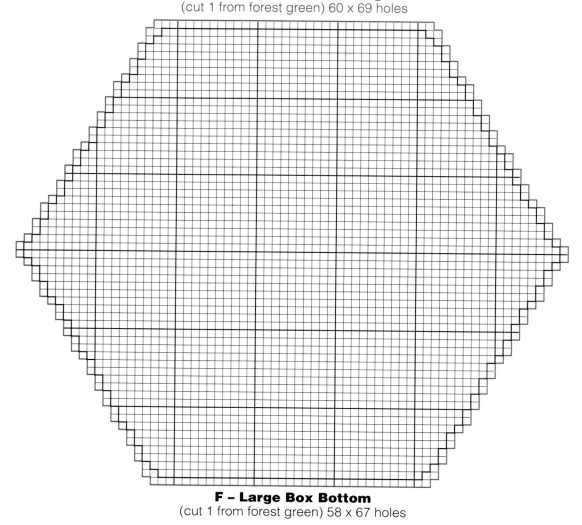

F – Large Box Bottom
(cut 1 from forest green) 58 x 67 holes

holy beginnings

noel
wreath

noel wreath

designed by
Mary Layfield

skill level & size

Challenging skill level. About 24" across [61cm], assembled.

materials

- 2½ sheets of 10-count plastic canvas
- Scrap of 7-count plastic canvas
- Desired colors, shapes and sizes of foil-backed acrylic gemstones
- Three 8" [20.3cm] lengths of brown cloth-covered wire
- One 24" [61cm] grapevine wreath
- 6 yds. [5.5m] of plaid 2½" [6.4cm] wire-edged ribbon
- Craft glue or glue gun
- Metallic cord; for amount see General Color Key.
- #16 metallic braid or metallic cord; for amount see General Color Key.
- #3 perle coton or six-strand embroidery floss; for amounts see General Color Key.

NOTE: A General Color Key has been provided to show complete yardage amounts; For easier stitching, separate Color Keys have been provided for each graph.

cutting instructions

NOTES: Use 7-count for H and 10-count canvas for remaining pieces.

A: For creche, cut one according to graph.
B: For king #1, cut one according to graph.
C: For king #2, cut one according to graph.
D: For king #3, cut one according to graph.
E: For shepherd #1, cut one according to graph.
F: For shepherd #2, cut one according to graph.
G: For shepherd #3, cut one according to graph.
H: For star, cut one according to graph.

stitching instructions

1: Using colors and stitches indicated, work A-H pieces according to graphs. With white for halos on creche and with matching colors, Overcast edges.

GENERAL COLOR KEY: Noel Wreath

Metallic cord				AMOUNT
Gold				9 yds. [8.2m]

#16 metallic braid or cord		Kreinik		AMOUNT
Gold		#002		6 yds. [5.5m]

#3 perle coton or floss	DMC®	Anchor®	JPC	AMOUNT
White	White	#2	#1001	11 yds. [10.1m]
Vy. Lt. Sky Blue	#747	#158	#7053	9 yds. [8.2m]
Lt. Turquoise	#598	#167	#7167	8 yds. [7.3m]
Vy. Dk. Coffee Brown	#898	#360	#5476	8 yds. [7.3m]
Lt. Brown	#434	#310	#5000	7 yds. [6.4m]
Med. Violet	#552	#99	#4092	7 yds. [6.4m]
Dk. Garnet	#814	#45	#3044	6 yds. [5.5m]
Dk. Salmon	#3328	#1024	#3071	6 yds. [5.5m]
Lt. Green	#701	#227	#6226	6 yds. [5.5m]
Med. Topaz	#783	#307	#5307	6 yds. [5.5m]
Peacock Blue	#807	#168	#7168	6 yds. [5.5m]
Off White	#746	#275	#2275	5 yds. [4.6m]
Sky Blue	#519	#1038	#7159	5 yds. [4.6m]
Vy. Lt. Topaz	#727	#293	#2289	5 yds. [4.6m]
Dk. Aquamarine	#991	#189	#6212	4 yds. [3.7m]
Dk. Terra Cotta	#355	#1014	#2339	4 yds. [3.7m]
Med. Blue	#826	#161	#7180	4 yds. [3.7m]
Med. Yellow Beige	#3046	#887	#2410	4 yds. [3.7m]
Vy. Lt. Mahogany	#402	#1047	#2306	4 yds. [3.7m]
Dk. Royal Blue	#796	#133	#7100	3 yds. [2.7m]
Lt. Tan	#437	#362	#5942	3 yds. [2.7m]
Navy Blue	#336	#150	#7981	3 yds. [2.7m]
Topaz	#725	#305	#2294	3 yds. [2.7m]
Vy. Dk. Violet	#550	#102	#4107	3 yds. [2.7m]
Vy. Lt. Golden Yellow	#3078	#292	#2292	3 yds. [2.7m]
Lt. Beige Brown	#841	#378	#5376	2 yds. [1.8m]
Lt. Pale Yellow	#745	#300	#2296	2 yds. [1.8m]
Ultra Dk. Pistachio Green	#890	#218	#6021	2 yds. [1.8m]
Black	#310	#403	#8403	1 yd. [0.9m]
Dk. Pewter Gray	#413	#401	#8514	1 yd. [0.9m]
Peach	#353	#8	#3006	1 yd. [0.9m]
Plum	#718	#88	#4089	1 yd. [0.9m]
Vy. Dk. Shell Pink	#221	#897	#3243	1 yd. [0.9m]
Vy. Lt. Peach	#948	#1011	#2331	1 yd. [0.9m]
Med. Nile Green	#913	#204	#6225	½ yd. [0.5m]
Vy. Lt. Pearl Gray	#762	#234	#8510	½ yd. [0.5m]

holy beginnings

2: Using black and embroidery stitches indicated, embroider facial detail on A-G pieces as indicated on graphs.

3: Glue gemstones to B-D pieces as desired or as shown in photo.

4: For each staff (make 3), bend end of one floral wire according to Wire Shaping Illustration. Glue one staff to wrong side of each

Shepherd's hand as shown.

NOTE: Cut ribbon into two 3-yd. [2.7m] lengths.

5: Beginning at top back of wreath, wrap one ribbon around wreath as shown; glue ends to back to secure.

6: Leaving a 12" [30.5cm] tail at each end, shape remaining ribbon into a multi-loop bow; trim ends as desired. Glue bow to front of wreath.

7: Glue star to bow and figures to wreath as shown. ✴

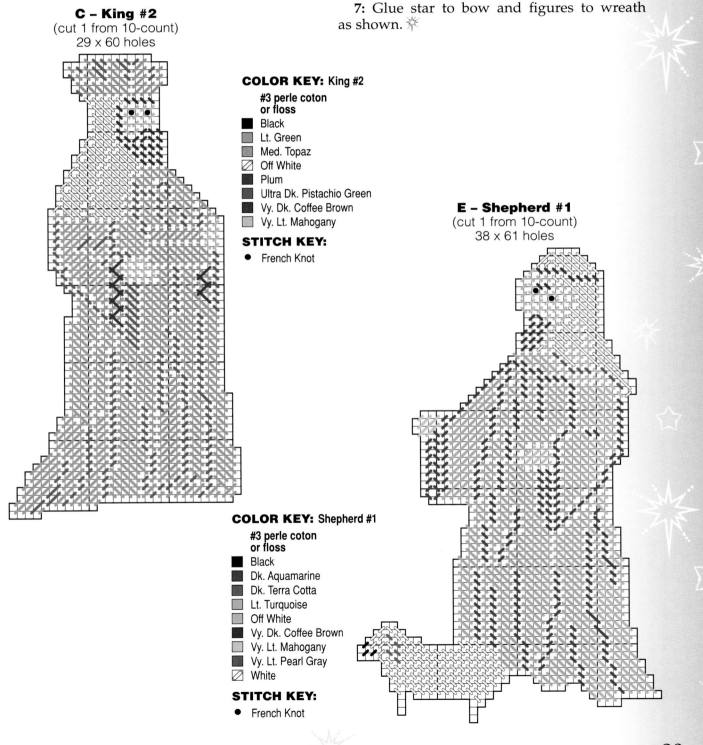

C – King #2
(cut 1 from 10-count)
29 x 60 holes

COLOR KEY: King #2
#3 perle coton or floss
- ■ Black
- ▨ Lt. Green
- ▨ Med. Topaz
- ▨ Off White
- ■ Plum
- ■ Ultra Dk. Pistachio Green
- ■ Vy. Dk. Coffee Brown
- ▨ Vy. Lt. Mahogany

STITCH KEY:
- ● French Knot

E – Shepherd #1
(cut 1 from 10-count)
38 x 61 holes

COLOR KEY: Shepherd #1
#3 perle coton or floss
- ■ Black
- ■ Dk. Aquamarine
- ■ Dk. Terra Cotta
- ▨ Lt. Turquoise
- ▨ Off White
- ■ Vy. Dk. Coffee Brown
- ▨ Vy. Lt. Mahogany
- ▨ Vy. Lt. Pearl Gray
- ▨ White

STITCH KEY:
- ● French Knot

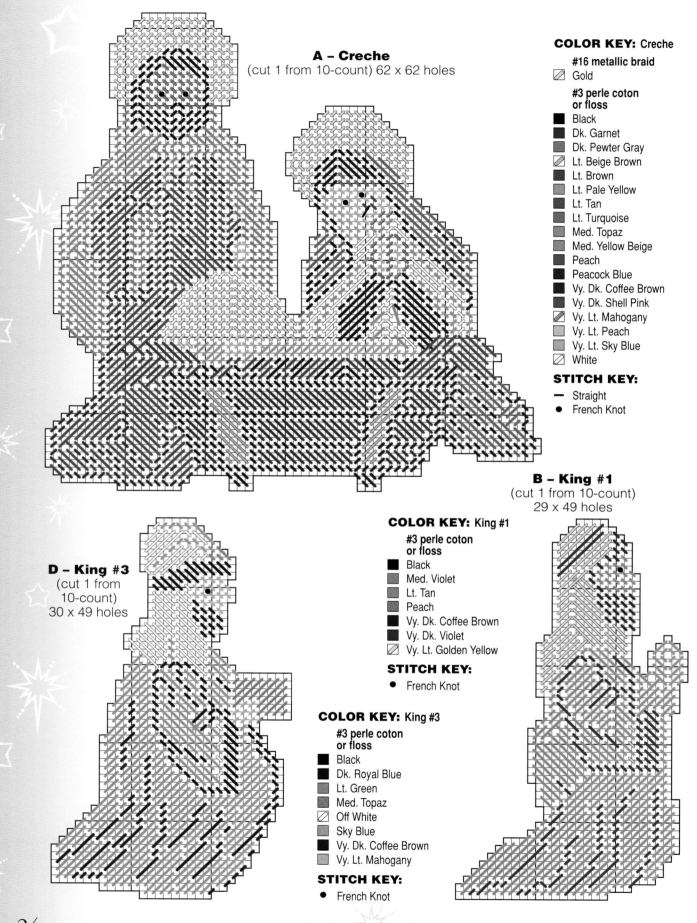

A – Creche
(cut 1 from 10-count) 62 x 62 holes

COLOR KEY: Creche

#16 metallic braid
- ▨ Gold

#3 perle coton or floss
- ■ Black
- ■ Dk. Garnet
- ▨ Dk. Pewter Gray
- ▨ Lt. Beige Brown
- ■ Lt. Brown
- ▨ Lt. Pale Yellow
- ▨ Lt. Tan
- ▨ Lt. Turquoise
- ▨ Med. Topaz
- ▨ Med. Yellow Beige
- ■ Peach
- ■ Peacock Blue
- ■ Vy. Dk. Coffee Brown
- ■ Vy. Dk. Shell Pink
- ▨ Vy. Lt. Mahogany
- ▨ Vy. Lt. Peach
- ▨ Vy. Lt. Sky Blue
- ▨ White

STITCH KEY:
- — Straight
- ● French Knot

B – King #1
(cut 1 from 10-count)
29 x 49 holes

COLOR KEY: King #1

#3 perle coton or floss
- ■ Black
- ▨ Med. Violet
- ▨ Lt. Tan
- ▨ Peach
- ■ Vy. Dk. Coffee Brown
- ■ Vy. Dk. Violet
- ▨ Vy. Lt. Golden Yellow

STITCH KEY:
- ● French Knot

D – King #3
(cut 1 from 10-count)
30 x 49 holes

COLOR KEY: King #3

#3 perle coton or floss
- ■ Black
- ■ Dk. Royal Blue
- ▨ Lt. Green
- ▨ Med. Topaz
- ▨ Off White
- ▨ Sky Blue
- ■ Vy. Dk. Coffee Brown
- ▨ Vy. Lt. Mahogany

STITCH KEY:
- ● French Knot

holy beginnings

**Wire Shaping
Illustration**

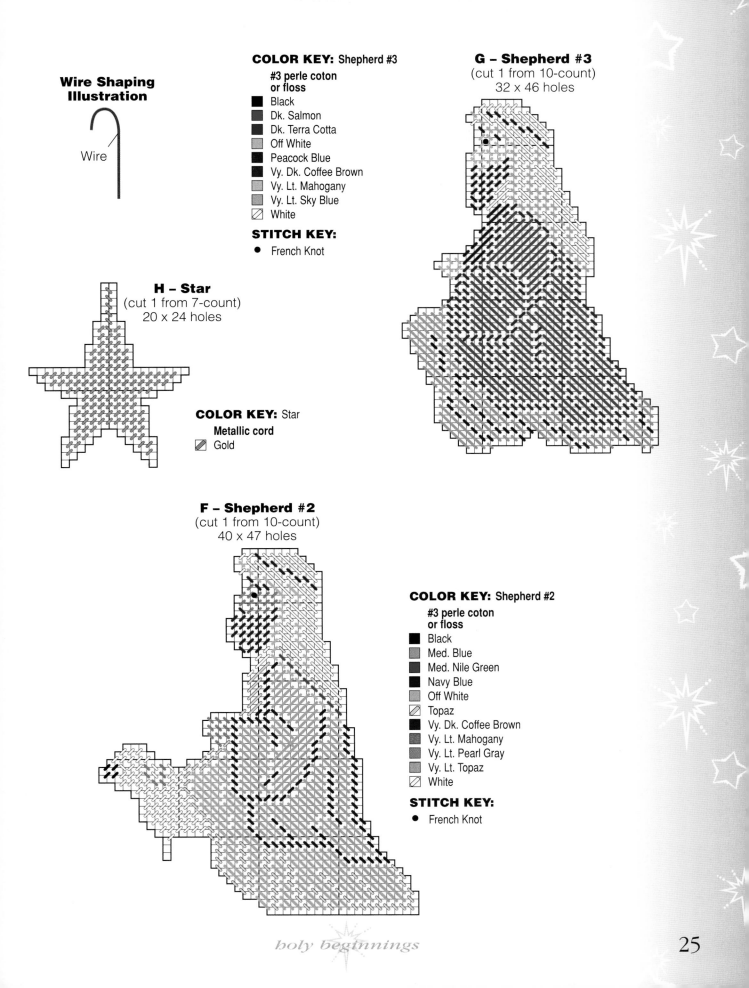

Wire

COLOR KEY: Shepherd #3

**#3 perle coton
or floss**

- ■ Black
- ■ Dk. Salmon
- ■ Dk. Terra Cotta
- ▨ Off White
- ■ Peacock Blue
- ■ Vy. Dk. Coffee Brown
- ▨ Vy. Lt. Mahogany
- ▨ Vy. Lt. Sky Blue
- ▨ White

STITCH KEY:

- ● French Knot

G – Shepherd #3
(cut 1 from 10-count)
32 x 46 holes

H – Star
(cut 1 from 7-count)
20 x 24 holes

COLOR KEY: Star

Metallic cord
- ▨ Gold

F – Shepherd #2
(cut 1 from 10-count)
40 x 47 holes

COLOR KEY: Shepherd #2

**#3 perle coton
or floss**

- ■ Black
- ▨ Med. Blue
- ■ Med. Nile Green
- ■ Navy Blue
- ▨ Off White
- ▨ Topaz
- ■ Vy. Dk. Coffee Brown
- ▨ Vy. Lt. Mahogany
- ▨ Vy. Lt. Pearl Gray
- ▨ Vy. Lt. Topaz
- ▨ White

STITCH KEY:

- ● French Knot

holy beginnings

designed by
Debbie Tabor

nativity
tissue cover

skill level & size

Average skill level. Loosely covers a 5¼" x 10" x 3¼" tall [13.3cm x 25.4cm x 8.3cm] oblong tissue box.

materials

- Two sheets of 7-count plastic canvas
- Velcro® closure (optional)
- Six-strand embroidery floss; for amounts see Color Key.
- Worsted-weight or plastic canvas yarn; for amounts see Color Key.

cutting instructions

A: For front and back, cut two (one for front and one for back) 21 x 65 holes.

B: For sides, cut two 21 x 34 holes (no graph).

C: For top, cut one according to graph.

D: For optional tissue cover bottom and flap, cut one 34 x 65 holes for bottom and one 12 x 65 holes for flap (no graphs).

stitching instructions

NOTE: D pieces are not worked.

1: Using colors and stitches indicated, work one A for front as indicated on graph. Using lilac and Continental Stitch, work remaining A for back, B and C pieces.

2: Using floss in colors and embroidery stitches indicated, embroider detail on front A as indicated on graph. With lilac, Overcast cutout edges of C.

3: With lilac, Whipstitch A-D pieces wrong sides together according to Nativity Tissue Cover Assembly Diagram; Overcast unfinished edges. ✷

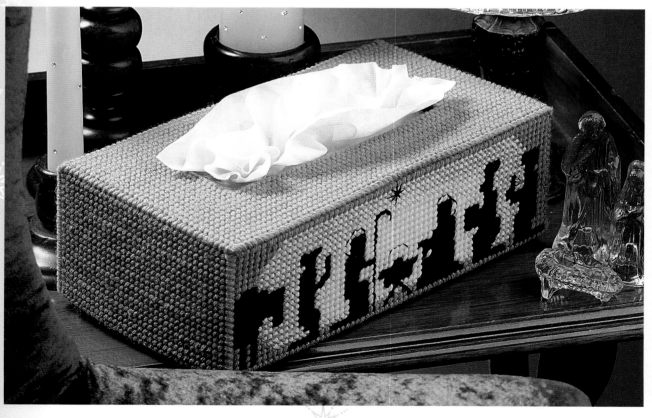

A – Front & Back
(cut 1 each) 21 x 65 holes

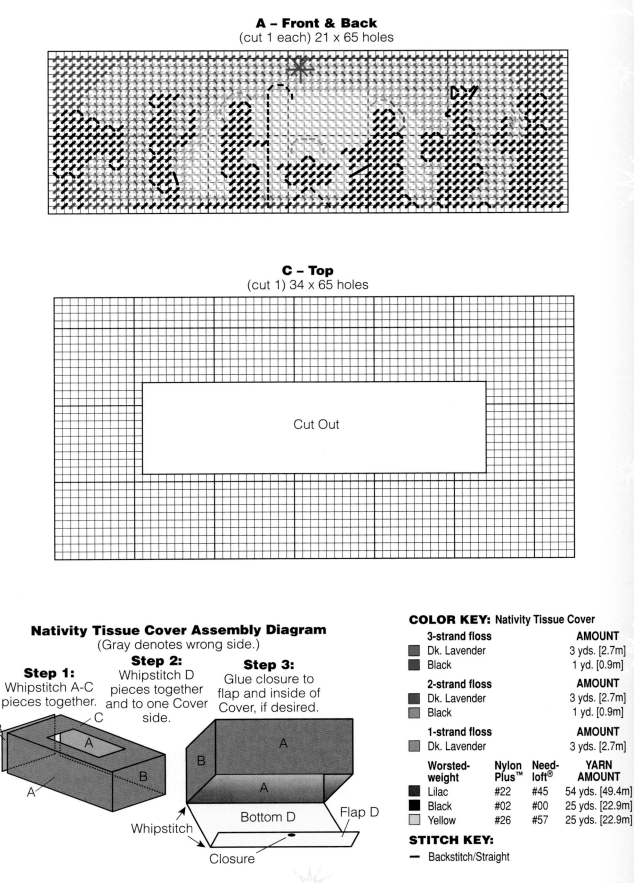

C – Top
(cut 1) 34 x 65 holes

Cut Out

Nativity Tissue Cover Assembly Diagram
(Gray denotes wrong side.)

Step 1:
Whipstitch A-C pieces together.

Step 2:
Whipstitch D pieces together and to one Cover side.

Step 3:
Glue closure to flap and inside of Cover, if desired.

B

C

A

B

A

A

B

A

A

Bottom D

Flap D

Whipstitch

Closure

COLOR KEY: Nativity Tissue Cover

3-strand floss		AMOUNT
Dk. Lavender		3 yds. [2.7m]
Black		1 yd. [0.9m]

2-strand floss		AMOUNT
Dk. Lavender		3 yds. [2.7m]
Black		1 yd. [0.9m]

1-strand floss		AMOUNT
Dk. Lavender		3 yds. [2.7m]

Worsted-weight	Nylon Plus™	Need-loft®	YARN AMOUNT
Lilac	#22	#45	54 yds. [49.4m]
Black	#02	#00	25 yds. [22.9m]
Yellow	#26	#57	25 yds. [22.9m]

STITCH KEY:
— Backstitch/Straight

holy beginnings

Tiptoe through our neighborhood of snow friends and meet Mr. and Mrs. Snow, a very lovely couple, gleeful little snowbirds, competing for the best snow angel, and a very helpful reindeer, poised to point the way to holiday fun.

snow friends

designed by
**Christine A.
Hendricks**

snow angel contest

skill level & size

Average skill level. 13¼" x 17⅜" [33.7cm x 44.1cm].

materials

- One 13½" x 22½" [34.3cm x 57.2cm] sheet of 7-count plastic canvas
- Six-strand embroidery floss; for amount see Color Key.
- Worsted-weight or plastic canvas yarn; for amounts see Color Key.

cutting instructions

For Snow Angel Contest, cut one 88 x 115 holes.

stitching instructions

1: Using colors and stitches indicated, work according to graph; fill in uncoded areas using white and Continental Stitch. With white, Overcast edges.

2: Using three strands black floss and embroidery stitches indicated, embroider detail as indicated on graph.

3: Hang or display as desired. ✳

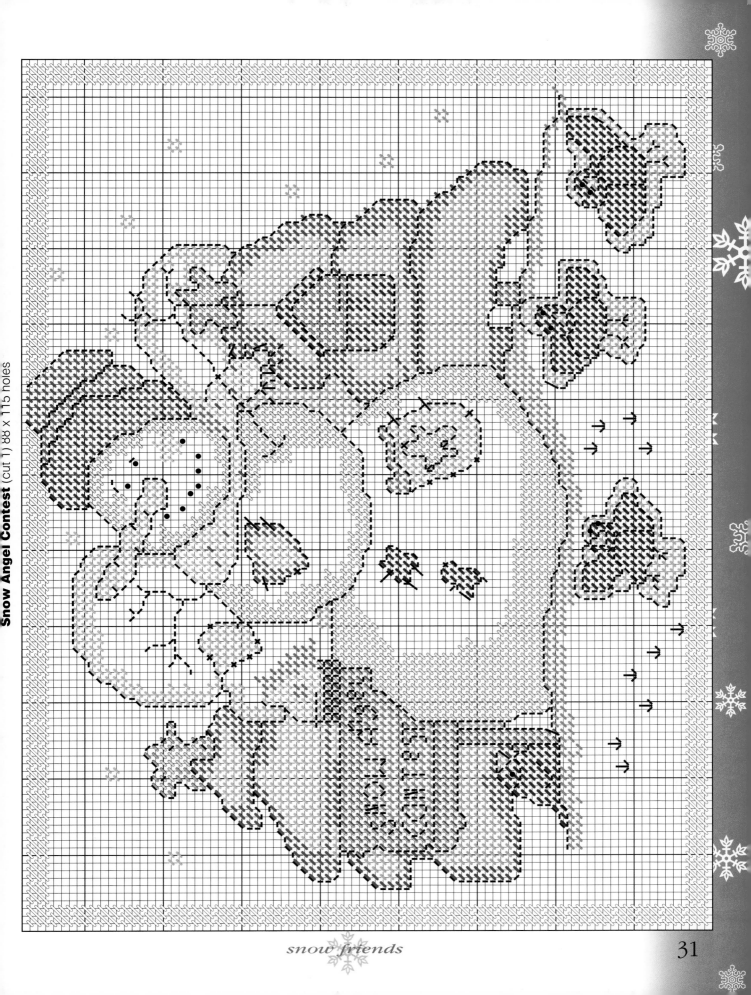

snow friends

designed by
Kimberly A.
Suber

snowman *basket*

skill level & size

Average skill level. 3½" x 7⅛" x 7½" tall [8.9cm x 18.1cm x 19.1cm].

materials

- Two sheets of 7-count plastic canvas
- 12 iridescent white ⅜" [20mm] round sequins
- ⅓ yd. [0.3m] gold metallic cord
- Craft glue or glue gun
- Worsted-weight or plastic canvas yarn; for amounts see Color Key.

cutting instructions

A: For basket front, cut one according to graph.

A – Basket Front
(cut 1) 47 x 50 holes

B: For basket sides, cut two 21 x 23 holes.
C: For basket back, cut one 21 x 47 holes.
D: For basket bottom, cut one 23 x 47 holes (no graph).
E: For snowman arms, cut two according to graph.
F: For wreath, cut one according to graph.
G: For holly leaves, cut two according to graph.
H: For holly berry, cut one 2 x 2 holes.

stitching instructions

NOTE: D is not worked.

1: Using colors and stitches indicated, work A-C and E-H pieces according to graphs. With matching colors, Overcast edges of E-H pieces.

2: Using colors and embroidery stitches indicated, embroider detail on A and F pieces as indicated on graphs.

3: With royal, Whipstitch A-D pieces together according to Basket Assembly Illustration; with royal for basket and with matching colors as shown in photo, Overcast unfinished edges.

4: Tie gold metallic cord into a small bow and trim ends as desired; glue bow to wreath as shown. Glue wreath and arms to snowman's body and holly leaves and berry to snowman's hat as shown. Glue sequins to basket front around snowman as desired or as shown. ❄

Basket Assembly Illustration
(Pieces are shown in different colors for contrast; gray denotes wrong side.)

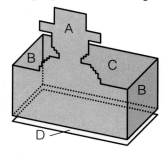

snow friends

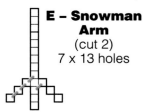

E – Snowman Arm
(cut 2)
7 x 13 holes

F – Wreath
(cut 1)
13 x 13 holes

Cut Out

G – Holly Leaf
(cut 2)
3 x 3 holes

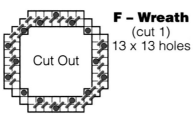

H – Holly Berry
(cut 1)
2 x 2 holes

B – Basket Side
(cut 2) 21 x 23 holes

C – Basket Back
(cut 1) 21 x 47 holes

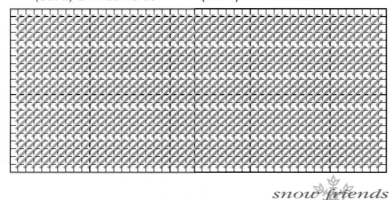

COLOR KEY: Snowman Basket

	Worsted-weight	Nylon Plus™	Need-loft®	YARN AMOUNT
	Sail Blue	#04	#35	38 yds. [34.7m]
	White	#01	#41	18 yds. [16.5m]
	Royal	#09	#32	10 yds. [9.1m]
	Black	#02	#00	7 yds. [6.4m]
	Red	#20	#01	5 yds. [4.6m]
	Xmas Green	#58	#28	3 yds. [2.7m]
	Maple	#35	#13	2 yds. [1.8m]
	Bright Orange	#17	#58	1 yd. [0.9m]
	Gold	#27	#17	1 yd. [0.9m]
	Pink	#11	#07	1 yd. [0.9m]

STITCH KEY:

— Backstitch/Straight
● French Knot

snow friends

snow friends

wintery night
wall decor

designed by
Kimberly A.
Suber

skill level & size

Average skill level. 10⅜" x 12⅞" [26.4cm x 32.7cm].

materials

- Two sheets of 7-count plastic canvas
- Craft glue or glue gun
- Worsted-weight or plastic canvas yarn; for amounts see Color Key.

cutting instructions

A: For base, cut one 69 x 85 holes.

B: For snowman pieces #1-#3, cut one each according to graphs.

C: For snowman hat, cut one according to graph.

D: For snowman arms, cut two according to graph.

E: For snowman scarf pieces #1 and #2, cut one according to graph for piece #1 and two 3 x 11 holes for pieces #2.

F: For snowman buttons, cut five 2 x 2 holes.

G: For birds #1 and #2, cut one each according to graphs.

H: For bird wings, cut two according to graph.

I: For trees #1 and #2, cut one each according to graphs.

J: For tree trunk, cut one 4 x 6 holes.

K: For small and large stars, cut number indicated according to graphs.

L: For moon, cut one according to graph.

stitching instructions

1: Using colors and stitches indicated, work pieces according to graphs. With royal for base, white for tree upper branches (see photo), tangerine for bird beaks and with matching colors, Overcast edges of pieces.

2: Using colors and embroidery stitches indicated, embroider detail on B#1, E and G pieces as indicated on graphs; using white and French Knot, randomly embroider snow on base (see photo).

NOTE: Cut six 4" [10.2cm] lengths of red.

3: For scarf fringe, attach one 4" strand with a Lark's Head Knot to each ▲ hole on each E#2 as indicated; trim and fray ends to fluff.

4: Glue pieces together and to base as shown. Hang or display as desired. ✳

COLOR KEY: Wintery Night Wall Decor

Worsted-weight	Nylon Plus™	Need-loft®	YARN AMOUNT
Royal	#09	#32	79 yds. [72.2m]
White	#01	#41	46 yds. [42.1m]
Gold	#27	#17	17 yds. [15.5m]
Xmas Green	#58	#28	12 yds. [11m]
Red	#20	#01	9 yds. [8.2m]
Black	#02	#00	5 yds. [4.6m]
Cinnamon	#44	#14	3 yds. [2.7m]
Tangerine	#15	#11	1 yd. [0.9m]
Bright Orange	#17	#58	¼ yd. [0.2m]

STITCH KEY:

— Backstitch/Straight
● French Knot

B – Snowman Piece #1
(cut 1)
10 x 10 holes

B – Snowman Piece #3
(cut 1) 19 x 19 holes

B – Snowman Piece #2
(cut 1) 16 x 16 holes

snow friends

C – Snowman Hat
(cut 1) 8 x 15 holes

D – Snowman Arm
(cut 2)
5 x 13 holes

E – Snowman Scarf Piece #1
(cut 1) 4 x 10 holes

E – Snowman Scarf Piece #2
(cut 2)
3 x 11 holes

A – Base (cut 1) 69 x 85 holes

snow friends

COLOR KEY: Wintery Night Wall Decor

Worsted-weight	Nylon Plus™	Need-loft®	YARN AMOUNT
Royal	#09	#32	79 yds. [72.2m]
White	#01	#41	46 yds. [42.1m]
Gold	#27	#17	17 yds. [15.5m]
Xmas Green	#58	#28	12 yds. [11m]
Red	#20	#01	9 yds. [8.2m]
Black	#02	#00	5 yds. [4.6m]
Cinnamon	#44	#14	3 yds. [2.7m]
Tangerine	#15	#11	1 yd. [0.9m]
Bright Orange	#17	#58	1/4 yd. [0.2m]

STITCH KEY:

— Backstitch/Straight

● French Knot

J – Tree Trunk
(cut 1)
4 x 6 holes

I – Tree #1
(cut 1)
27 x 39 holes

I – Tree #2
(cut 1)
15 x 18 holes

F – Snowman Button
(cut 5)
2 x 2 holes

H – Bird Wing
(cut 2)
3 x 3 holes

G – Bird #1
(cut 1)
8 x 9 holes

G – Bird #2
(cut 1)
8 x 9 holes

Beak

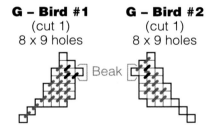

K – Large Star
(cut 3)
8 x 9 holes

K – Small Star
(cut 2)
5 x 6 holes

L – Moon
(cut 1)
10 x 13 holes

Holiday Tips

Try this delicious punch recipe. It's sure to put you in the holiday spirit.

Hot Cranberry Fruit Punch

Ingredients:

4 cups cranberry juice
2 cups orange juice
2 tbsps. lemon juice
2 tbsps. sugar
2 tsp. cinnamon
2 shakes of ground cloves

Directions:

Mix all ingredients; bring to a boil, lower temperature and simmer for twenty minutes. Enjoy.

mr. & mrs. *snowman*

designed by
Mary
Layfield

skill level & sizes

Challenging skill level. Mr. Snowman is about 10" across x 17" tall [25.4cm x 43.2cm], including hat; Mrs. Snowman is about 9" across x 14" tall [22.9cm x 35.6cm], including bonnet.

materials

- Eight sheets of 7-count plastic canvas
- Three Darice® 9½" [24.1cm] plastic canvas radial circles
- 1 yd. [0.9m] red 1" [2.5cm] and ½ yd. [0.5m] red 1¾" [4.4cm] eyelet ruffle
- 3" x 63" [7.6cm x 160cm] length of striped fabric
- Seven desired-color sew-on and four black shank-backed buttons
- One 20mm clear snowflake acrylic stone
- ¼ yd. [0.2m] wooden ¼" [6mm] dowel
- 20 or more 3" [7.6cm] lengths of straw from a broom
- ¼ yd. [0.2m] of silver metallic cord
- Two zip-lock bags filled with stuffing pellets or weighting material of choice
- Polyester fiberfill
- Craft glue or glue gun
- Worsted-weight or plastic canvas yarn; for amounts see Color Key on page 40.

cutting instructions

A: For Mr. Snowman body sides, cut four according to graph.

B: For Mr. Snowman head sides, cut four according to graph.

C: For Mr. Snowman hat brim pieces, cut two (one from each of two circles) according to graph; set aside one center for D.

D: For Mr. Snowman hat top, use center cut from one full circle according to C graph.

E: For Mr. Snowman hat side pieces, cut one 23 x 52 holes and one 23 x 56 holes (no graphs).

F: For Mrs. Snowman body sides, cut four according to graph.

G: For Mrs. Snowman head sides, cut

four according to graph.

H: For Mrs. Snowman bonnet brim, cut one from remaining circle according to graph.

I: For Mrs. Snowman bonnet top, cut one 8 x 54 holes.

J: For Mrs. Snowman bonnet back, cut one according to graph.

K: For Mr. & Mrs. Snowman arms, cut four according to graph.

L: For Mr. & Mrs. Snowman inner gloves, cut four according to graph.

M: For Mr. & Mrs. Snowman nose pieces, cut three each according to graphs.

N: For Mr. & Mrs. Snowman mouths, cut one each according to graphs.

O: For Mrs. Snowman purse sides, cut two 11 x 18 holes.

stitching instructions

1: Using colors and stitches (Leave ¼" [6mm] loops on Modified Turkey Work stitches; use a doubled strand of yarn for fuller coverage.) indicated, work A-D, F-M (two of each K and L and one of each M pieces on opposite side of canvas) and O pieces according to graphs; overlapping two holes at each end of each piece and working through both thicknesses at each overlap area to join, work E according to Hat Side Stitch Pattern Guide. With black, Overcast every other hole on each N piece (see photo).

2: For each arm (make 4), with Xmas red, Whipstitch one of each K and L pieces wrong sides together as indicated on graphs; with white, Overcast unfinished edges of K pieces.

3: For each snowman (make 2), with white, Whipstitch and assemble corresponding body sides, corresponding head sides, two arms, weighting material and fiberfill according to Snowman Assembly Diagram.

4: With black, Whipstitch C-E pieces together according to Hat Assembly Diagram. Whipstitch and assemble H-J pieces and eyelet ruffles as indicated and according to

Bonnet Assembly Diagram.

5: For each nose, with orange, Whipstitch corresponding M pieces wrong sides together as indicated; Overcast unfinished edges.

NOTE: Cut one 1½"-square [3.8cm] piece of fabric.

6: Glue fabric square and snowflake stone to hat and hat to Mr. Snowman's head as shown in photo. Glue two shank-backed buttons and corresponding nose and mouth to each head as shown; glue three or more flat buttons to each body as shown.

7: Hold broom straws together and around one end of dowel; wrap Xmas red yarn around straw and dowel to secure; secure ends of yarn under wraps, forming broom. Glue, or with Xmas red, tack broom to Mr. Snowman's glove as shown.

8: For purse, tie a knot in each end of metallic cord. Holding O pieces wrong sides together with knots of cord between (see photo), with black, Whipstitch together. Place purse over one glove on Mrs. Snowman; glue to secure.

NOTE: Cut one 3" x 31" [7.6cm x 78.7cm] and one 3" x 26" [7.6cm x 66cm] strip of fabric.

9: For each snowman (use long strip for Mr. Snowman and short strip for Mrs. Snowman), wrap fabric around neck. Tie ends of long strip together at front of Mr. Snowman as shown; glue ends of short strip to Mrs. Snowman's gloves as shown. Place bonnet over Mrs. Snowman's head and tie ruffle ends into a bow at front as shown. ❈

COLOR KEY: Mr. & Mrs. Snowman

	Worsted-weight	Nylon Plus™	Need-loft®	YARN AMOUNT
	White	#01	#41	8 oz. [226.8g]
	Black	#02	#00	3 oz. [85.1g]
	Xmas Red	#19	#02	66 yds. [60.4m]
	Sail Blue	#04	#35	37 yds. [33.8m]
	Bright Orange	#17	#58	9 yds. [8.2m]

STITCH KEY:
- ✑ Modified Turkey Work

A – Mr. Snowman Body Side
(cut 4) 38 x 67 holes

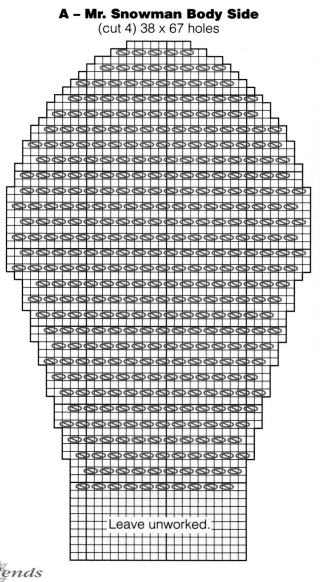

B – Mr. Snowman Head Side
(cut 4) 31 x 49 holes

**F – Mrs. Snowman
Body Side**
(cut 4) 34 x 59 holes

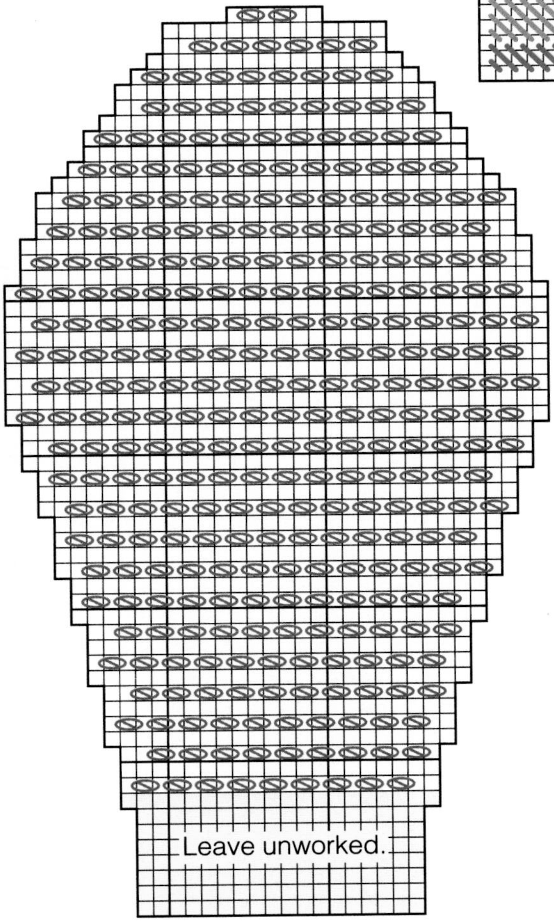

Leave unworked.

I – Mrs. Snowman Bonnet Top (cut 1) 8 x 54 holes

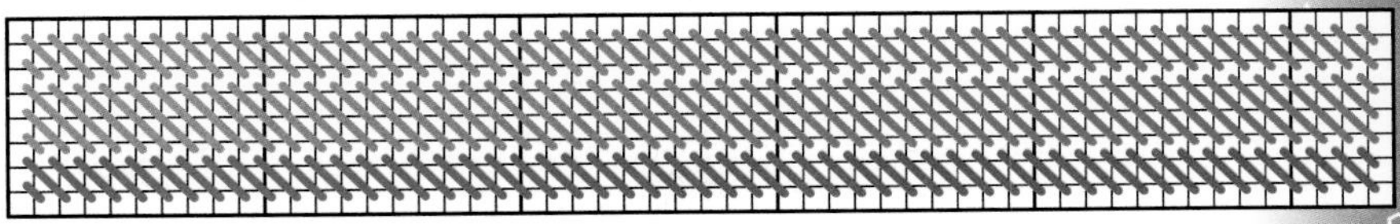

**J – Mrs. Snowman
Bonnet Back**
(cut 1) 20 x 21 holes

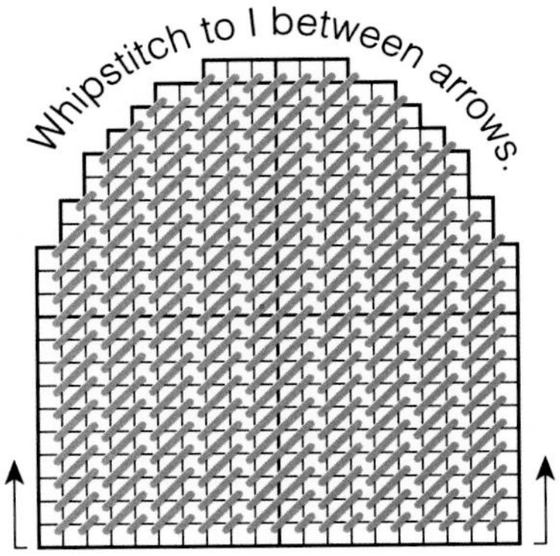

Whipstitch to I between arrows.

**G – Mrs. Snowman
Head Side**
(cut 4) 20 x 34 holes

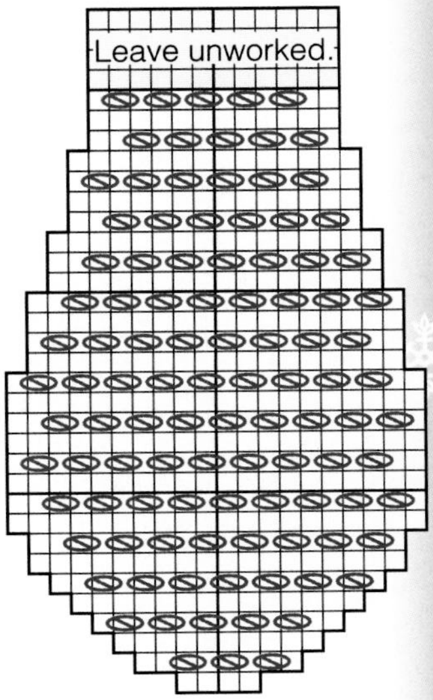

Leave unworked.

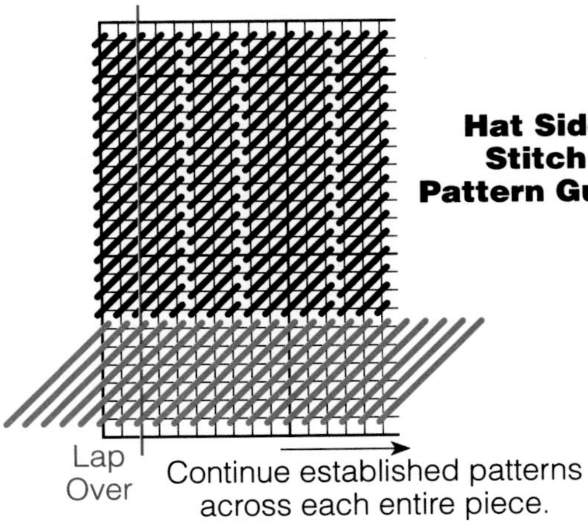

**Hat Side
Stitch
Pattern Guide**

Lap
Over

Continue established patterns
across each entire piece.

**K – Mr. & Mrs.
Snowman Arm**
(cut 4)
41 x 44 holes

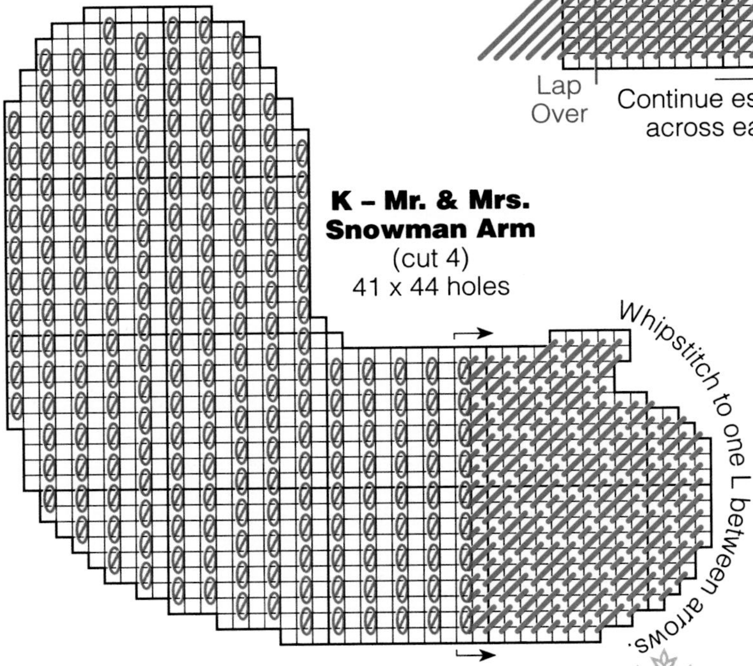

Whipstitch to one L between arrows.

**L – Mr. & Mrs. Snowman
Inner Glove**
(cut 4) 16 x 20 holes

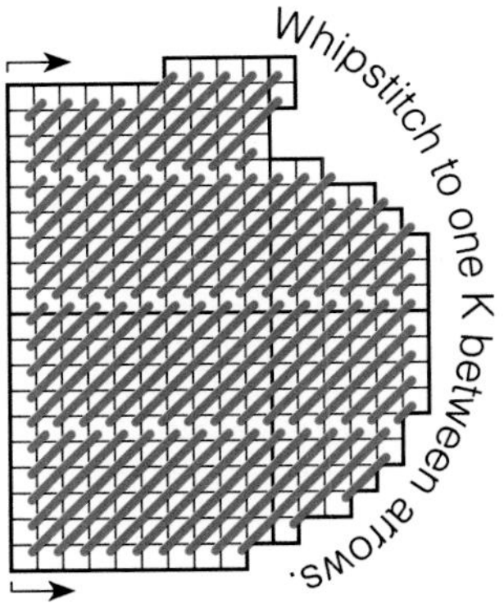

Whipstitch to one K between arrows.

H – Mrs. Snowman Bonnet Brim
(cut 1)

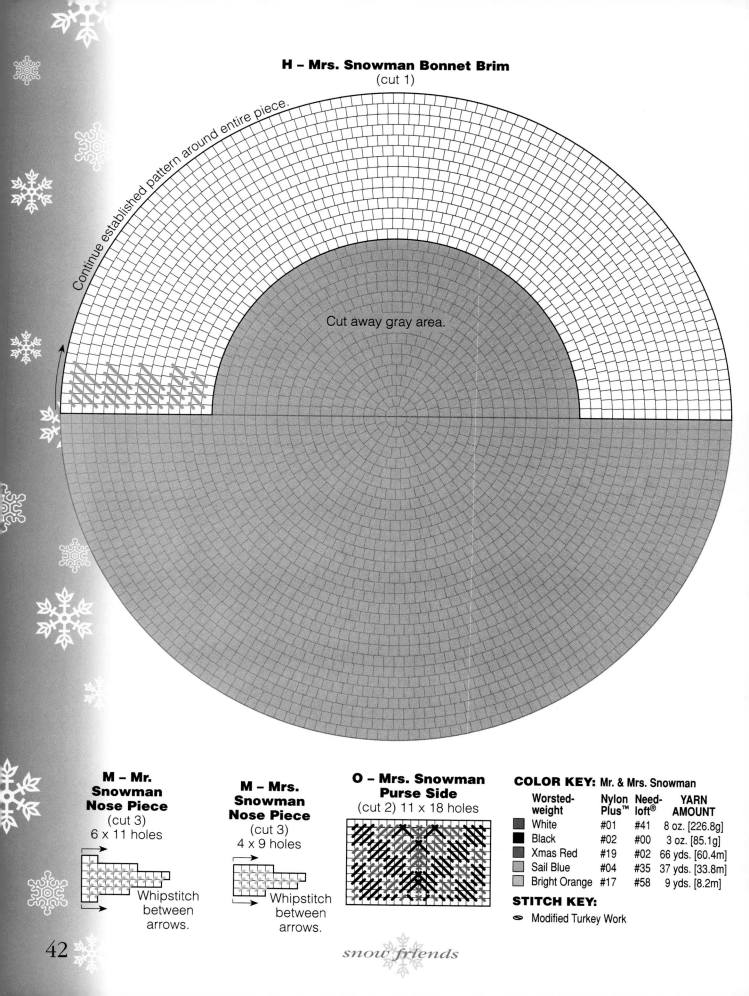

Continue established pattern around entire piece.

Cut away gray area.

M – Mr. Snowman Nose Piece
(cut 3)
6 x 11 holes

Whipstitch between arrows.

M – Mrs. Snowman Nose Piece
(cut 3)
4 x 9 holes

Whipstitch between arrows.

O – Mrs. Snowman Purse Side
(cut 2) 11 x 18 holes

COLOR KEY: Mr. & Mrs. Snowman

Worsted-weight	Nylon Plus™	Need-loft®	YARN AMOUNT
White	#01	#41	8 oz. [226.8g]
Black	#02	#00	3 oz. [85.1g]
Xmas Red	#19	#02	66 yds. [60.4m]
Sail Blue	#04	#35	37 yds. [33.8m]
Bright Orange	#17	#58	9 yds. [8.2m]

STITCH KEY:
◓ Modified Turkey Work

snow friends

C – Mr. Snowman Hat Brim Piece
(cut 2)

Continue established pattern around each entire piece.

D – Mr. Snowman Hat Top
(cut 1)

Cut out gray area.

N – Mr. Snowman Mouth
(cut 1)
6 x 19 holes

N – Mrs. Snowman Mouth
(cut 1)
4 x 11 holes

Bonnet Assembly Diagram
(Pieces are shown in different colors for contrast; gray denotes wrong side.)

Step 1:
With sail blue, Whipstitch H-J pieces together.

Step 2:
With Xmas red for bonnet brim and with sail blue, Overcast unfinished edges.

Wide Ruffle

Narrow Ruffle

Step 3:
Glue wide ruffle to underside of bonnet; glue narrow ruffle to top and around sides of bonnet, leaving remaining ends loose for ties.

Hat Assembly Diagram
(Pieces are shown in different colors for contrast; lt. gray denotes wrong side.)

Step 1:
Whipstitch outer edges of C pieces together.

Step 2:
Whipstitch D and E pieces together; Whipstitch E pieces to cutout edges of C pieces through both thicknesses.

Snowman Assembly Diagram
(Pieces are shown in different colors for contrast; gray denotes wrong side.)

Step 1:
Whipstitch corresponding body sides together, leaving one seam edge open for assembly; repeat with corresponding head sides.

Body Side

Step 2:
Tack head and two arms to body.

Head

Arm

Body

Arm

Step 3:
(not shown)
Place weighting material in bottom of body and Whipstitch seam closed, stuffing remainder of body with fiberfill as you work.

Step 4:
(not shown)
Whipstitch head seam closed, stuffing head with fiberfill as you work.

snow friends

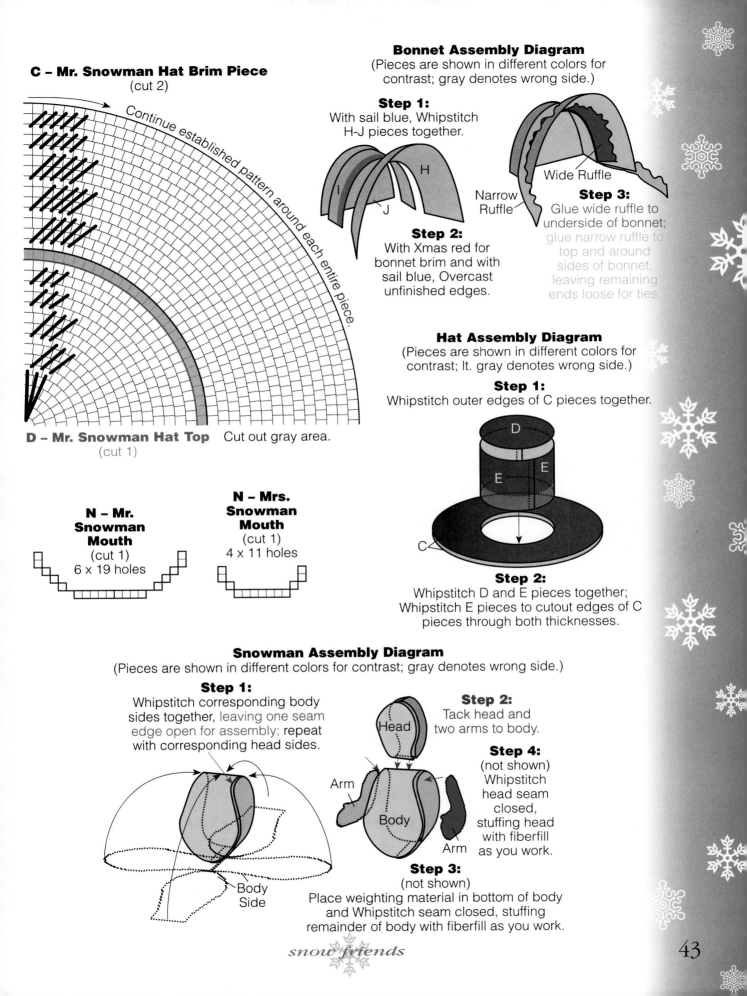

designed by
**Janelle Giese of
Janelle Marie
Designs**

merry winter *carolers*

skill level & sizes

Average skill level. Ornament #1 is 3" x 4¾"
[7.6cm x 12.1cm]; Ornament #2 is 2⅝" x 4⅜"
[6.7cm x 11.1cm]; Ornament #3 is 3⅜" x 3⅞"
[8.6cm x 9.8cm].

materials

- ½ sheet of 7-count plastic canvas
- #5 perle coton; for amount see Color Key.
- Six-strand embroidery floss; for amount see Color Key.
- Worsted-weight or plastic canvas yarn; for amounts see Color Key.

cutting instructions

A: For Ornament #1, cut one according to graph.
B: For Ornament #2, cut one according to graph.
C: For Ornament #3, cut one according to graph.

stitching instructions

1: Using colors indicated and Continental Stitch, work pieces according to graphs. With baby blue for bodies and with matching colors as shown in photo, Overcast edges of pieces.

2: Using perle coton, one strand floss and yarn in colors and embroidery stitches indicated, embroider detail (work eye stitches on

Ornaments #1 and #3 and mouth stitches on Ornament #3 six times) on pieces as indicated on graphs.

3: Hang or display as desired. ❄

A – Ornament #1
(cut 1) 20 x 31 holes

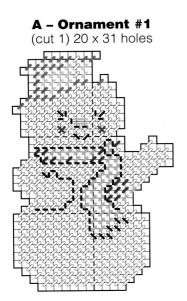

C – Ornament #3
(cut 1) 22 x 25 holes

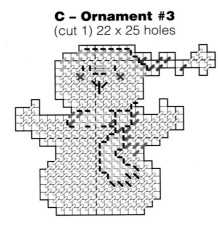

B – Ornament #2
(cut 1) 17 x 29 holes

This elegant treatment is easy to achieve with tissue paper, bleach and a rich tasseled cord.

Orchid Elegance Gift Wrap

Materials:
Colored tissue paper
Liquid bleach
Corded tassel

Instructions:
Iron tissue paper and place on protected surface. Pour ¼ cup bleach in a small bowl. Dip a toothbrush (for small spatters) or plastic mesh dish scrubber (for large spatters) into bleach and dribble and flick onto paper. Allow to dry. Iron paper if desired.

Wrap gift and tie tasseled cord in double knot around package.

COLOR KEY: Merry Winter Carolers

#5 perle coton	DMC®	AMOUNT
■ Black	#310	9 yds. [8.2m]

Embroidery floss	DMC®	AMOUNT
■ Med. Rose	#899	1 yd. [0.9m]

Worsted-weight	Nylon Plus™	Need-loft®	YARN AMOUNT
▨ White	#01	#41	18 yds. [16.5m]
☐ Baby Blue	#05	#36	5 yds. [4.6m]
▦ Crimson	#53	–	3 yds. [2.7m]
▨ Red	#20	#01	3 yds. [2.7m]
■ Royal Dark	#07	#48	3 yds. [2.7m]
▨ Royal	#09	#32	3 yds. [2.7m]
▨ Black	#02	#00	2 yds. [1.8m]
▨ Forest	#32	#29	1 yd. [0.9m]
▨ Watermelon	#54	#55	1 yd. [0.9m]
▨ Xmas Green	#58	#28	1 yd. [0.9m]

STITCH KEY:
— Backstitch/Straight
● French Knot
× Cross

designed by
**Candy
Clayton**

skill level & size

Easy skill level. Each is 10½" x 11" [26.7cm x 27.9cm].

materials

• Four sheets of 7-count plastic canvas

• Three red 5mm pom-poms
• Craft glue or glue gun
• Worsted-weight or plastic canvas yarn; for amounts see Color Key.

cutting instructions

A: For gentleman star front and backing, cut two (one for front and one for backing) according to graph.

B: For lady star front and backing, cut two (one for front and one for backing) according to graph.

C: For leaves, cut two according to graph.

D: For buttons, cut four according to graph.

**A – Gentleman Star
Front & Backing**
(cut 1 each)
70 x 74 holes

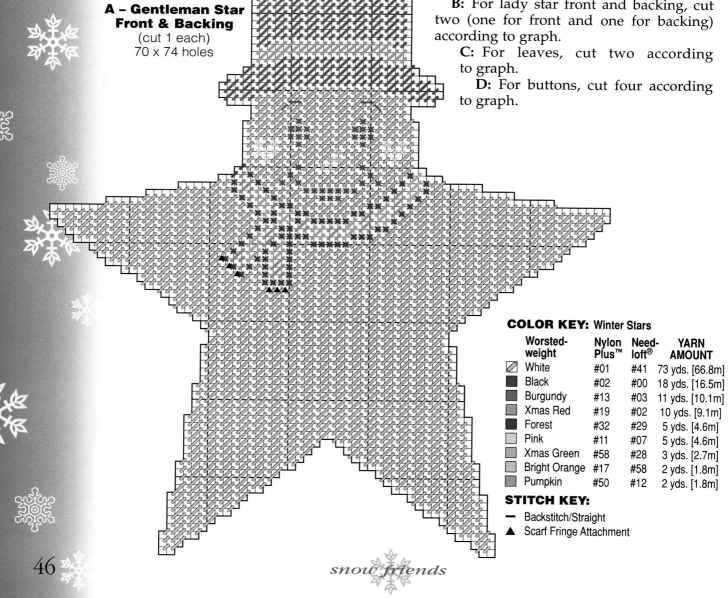

COLOR KEY: Winter Stars

	Worsted-weight	Nylon Plus™	Need-loft®	YARN AMOUNT
▨	White	#01	#41	73 yds. [66.8m]
■	Black	#02	#00	18 yds. [16.5m]
▨	Burgundy	#13	#03	11 yds. [10.1m]
▨	Xmas Red	#19	#02	10 yds. [9.1m]
■	Forest	#32	#29	5 yds. [4.6m]
▨	Pink	#11	#07	5 yds. [4.6m]
▨	Xmas Green	#58	#28	3 yds. [2.7m]
▨	Bright Orange	#17	#58	2 yds. [1.8m]
▨	Pumpkin	#50	#12	2 yds. [1.8m]

STITCH KEY:

— Backstitch/Straight
▲ Scarf Fringe Attachment

snow friends

stitching instructions

NOTE: One of each A and B pieces are not worked for backings.

1: Using colors and stitches indicated, work one A for front, one B for front, C and D pieces according to graphs; with matching colors, Overcast edges of C and D pieces.

2: Using colors (Separate into individual plies, if desired.) and embroidery stitches indicated, embroider facial detail on front A and front B pieces as indicated on graphs.

NOTE: Cut six 3" [7.6cm] lengths of Xmas green.

3: For scarf fringe, attach one 3" strand with a Lark's Head Knot to each ▲ hole on front A as indicated; trim and fray ends to fluff.

4: For each star, holding one backing to wrong side of corresponding front, with matching colors as shown in photo, Whipstitch together.

5: Glue leaves and pom-poms to gentleman's hat and two buttons to each star as shown. Hang or display as desired. ✳

COLOR KEY: Winter Stars

	Worsted-weight	Nylon Plus™	Need-loft®	YARN AMOUNT
▨	White	#01	#41	73 yds. [66.8m]
■	Black	#02	#00	18 yds. [16.5m]
■	Burgundy	#13	#03	11 yds. [10.1m]
▨	Xmas Red	#19	#02	10 yds. [9.1m]
■	Forest	#32	#29	5 yds. [4.6m]
▨	Pink	#11	#07	5 yds. [4.6m]
▨	Xmas Green	#58	#28	3 yds. [2.7m]
▨	Bright Orange	#17	#58	2 yds. [1.8m]
▨	Pumpkin	#50	#12	2 yds. [1.8m]

STITCH KEY:
- — Backstitch/Straight
- ▲ Scarf Fringe Attachment

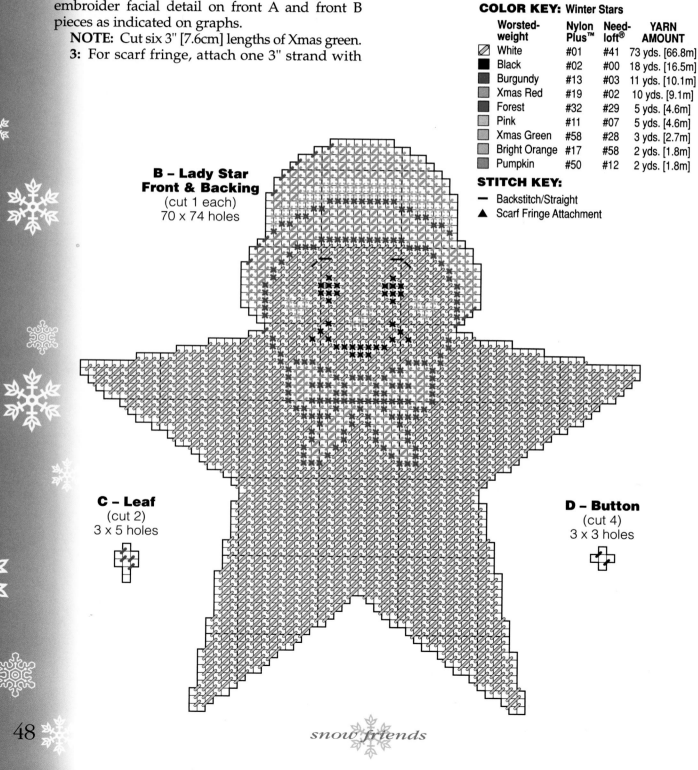

B – Lady Star Front & Backing
(cut 1 each)
70 x 74 holes

C – Leaf
(cut 2)
3 x 5 holes

D – Button
(cut 4)
3 x 3 holes

snow friends

reindeer sign

designed by
Robin Petrina

skill level & size

Average skill level. 10¾" x 22¾" [27.3cm x 57.8cm].

materials

- 2½ sheets of 7-count plastic canvas
- Craft glue or glue gun
- Worsted-weight or plastic canvas yarn; for amounts see Color Key on page 50.

cutting instructions

A: For reindeer head, cut one according to graph.

B: For reindeer body, cut one according to graph.

C: For reindeer front hooves, cut two according to graph.

D: For reindeer back hooves, cut two according to graph.

E: For reindeer eyes, cut two according to graph.

F: For reindeer nose, cut one according to graph.

G: For sign, cut one according to graph.

H: For light bulbs, cut three according to graph.

I: For letters, cut number needed to spell "The North Pole" according to graph.

stitching instructions

1: Using colors and stitches indicated, work A-H (substitute yellow for sail blue on one H and Xmas green for sail blue on remaining H) pieces according to graphs.

2: With camel for eyes, holly for letters and with matching colors, Overcast edges of A-F, H and I pieces. For sign, with white for stake

snow friends   49

edges and alternating red and white for platform edges (see photo), Overcast edges of G.

3: Using white and Straight Stitch, embroider eye highlights on E pieces as indicated on graph.

NOTE: Cut one 12" [30.5cm] length of Xmas green.

4: Leaving 3" [7.6cm] between bulbs and at ends of strand, thread strand from back to front, then from front to back through ♦ holes on each H piece as indicated. Glue bulbs and strand to stake of sign as desired or as shown in photo, gluing ends of strand to back to secure.

5: Glue pieces together as shown. ❋

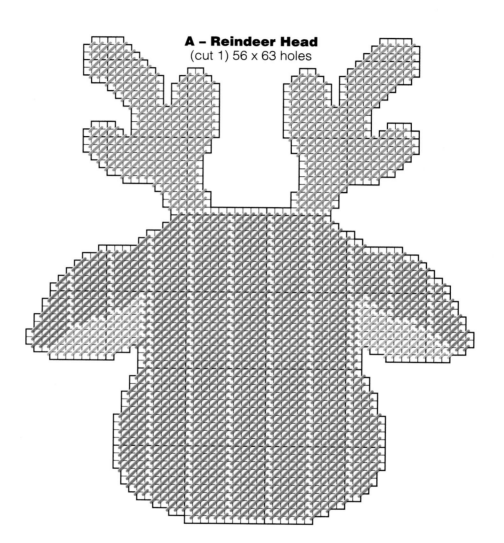

A – Reindeer Head
(cut 1) 56 x 63 holes

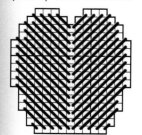

**D – Reindeer
Back Hoof**
(cut 2) 15 x 16 holes

**C – Reindeer
Front Hoof**
(cut 2) 12 x 15 holes

I – Letters
(cut number needed) 5 x 7 holes

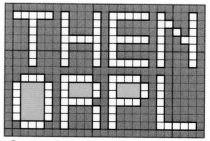

Cut out lt. yellow areas carefully.

snow friends

G – Sign (cut 1) 70 x 90 holes

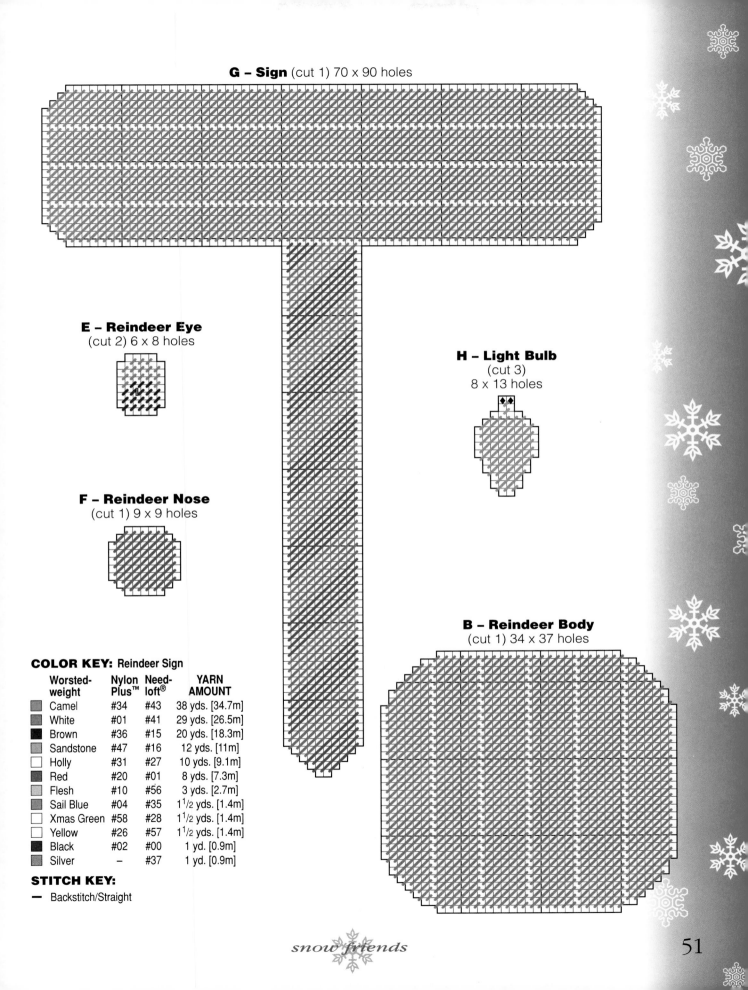

E – Reindeer Eye
(cut 2) 6 x 8 holes

H – Light Bulb
(cut 3)
8 x 13 holes

F – Reindeer Nose
(cut 1) 9 x 9 holes

B – Reindeer Body
(cut 1) 34 x 37 holes

COLOR KEY: Reindeer Sign

	Worsted-weight	Nylon Plus™	Need-loft®	YARN AMOUNT
	Camel	#34	#43	38 yds. [34.7m]
	White	#01	#41	29 yds. [26.5m]
	Brown	#36	#15	20 yds. [18.3m]
	Sandstone	#47	#16	12 yds. [11m]
	Holly	#31	#27	10 yds. [9.1m]
	Red	#20	#01	8 yds. [7.3m]
	Flesh	#10	#56	3 yds. [2.7m]
	Sail Blue	#04	#35	1½ yds. [1.4m]
	Xmas Green	#58	#28	1½ yds. [1.4m]
	Yellow	#26	#57	1½ yds. [1.4m]
	Black	#02	#00	1 yd. [0.9m]
	Silver	–	#37	1 yd. [0.9m]

STITCH KEY:

— Backstitch/Straight

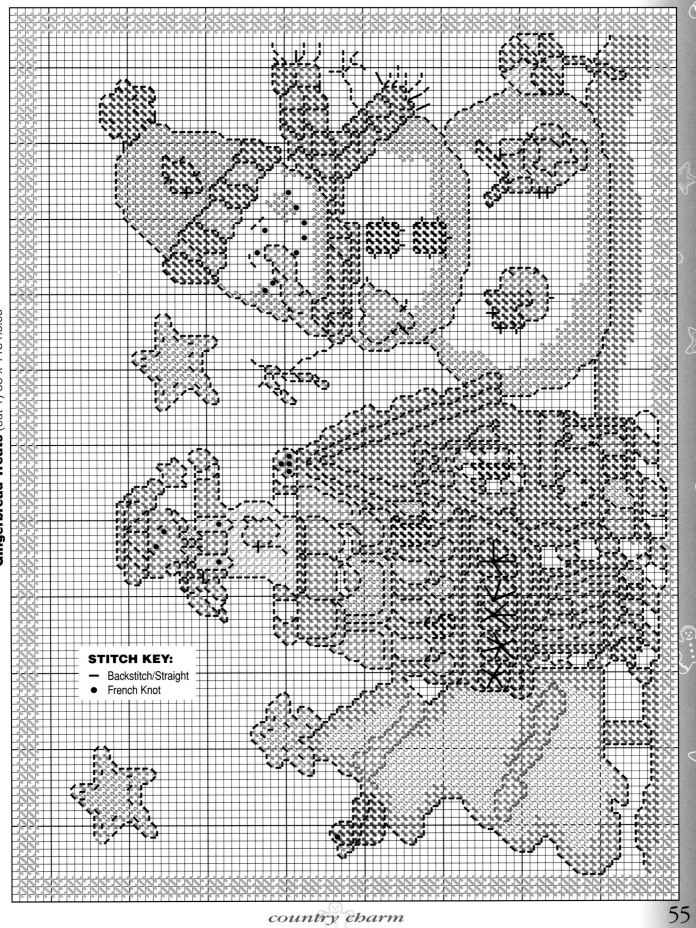

STITCH KEY:
— Backstitch/Straight
● French Knot

my *first* pony

designed by
Diane T. Ray

skill level & size

Challenging skill level. 3¼" x 9½" x 8½" tall [8.3cm x 24.1cm x 21.6cm].

materials

- Five sheets of 7-count plastic canvas
- Three red 10mm pom-poms
- 2¼"-across [5.7cm] bezel clock movement
- Eight 4½"-long [11.4cm] craft or ice cream sticks
- Metallic cord; for amount see Color Key on page 59.
- Worsted-weight or plastic canvas yarn; for amounts see Color Key.

cutting instructions

A: For outer side #1 and #2, cut one each according to graphs.

B: For inner side #1 and #2, cut one each according to graphs.

C: For top, cut one according to graph.

D: For back, cut one according to graph.

E: For bottom, cut one according to graph.

F: For chin, cut one 3 x 6 holes.

G: For muzzle, cut one 3 x 3 holes.

H: For brace pieces, cut four 5 x 17 holes.

I: For stirrup straps, cut two according to graph.

J: For stirrups, cut two according to graph.

K: For holly leaves, cut two according to graph.

stitching instructions

NOTES: J pieces are not worked.

If your metallic cord has a core, the core may be removed for easier stitching. To do so, cut a length of cord, grasp core fibers with fingertips or tweezers and pull. Core slips out easily.

1: Using colors and stitches indicated and leaving indicated and uncoded areas unworked, work A-I (leave 1" [2.5cm] mane ends and 5" [12.7cm] tail ends on Continuous Lark's Head Knot stitches) pieces according to graphs.

2: With holly for K and with matching colors

Pony Assembly Diagram

(Pieces are shown in different colors for contrast; gray denotes wrong side.)

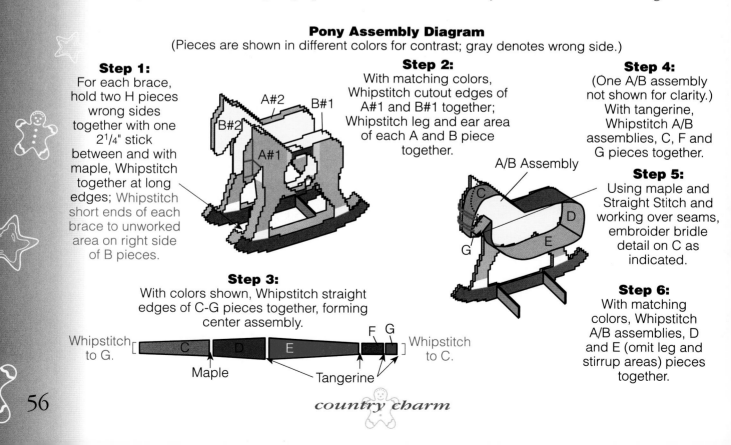

Step 1:
For each brace, hold two H pieces wrong sides together with one 2¼" stick between and with maple, Whipstitch together at long edges; Whipstitch short ends of each brace to unworked area on right side of B pieces.

Step 2:
With matching colors, Whipstitch cutout edges of A#1 and B#1 together; Whipstitch leg and ear area of each A and B piece together.

Step 3:
With colors shown, Whipstitch straight edges of C-G pieces together, forming center assembly.

Step 4:
(One A/B assembly not shown for clarity.) With tangerine, Whipstitch A/B assemblies, C, F and G pieces together.

Step 5:
Using maple and Straight Stitch and working over seams, embroider bridle detail on C as indicated.

Step 6:
With matching colors, Whipstitch A/B assemblies, D and E (omit leg and stirrup areas) pieces together.

and omitting attachment areas, Overcast edges of C, E, I and K pieces. Using colors (Separate into individual plies, if desired.) indicated and

Stirrup Assembly Diagram

Step 1:
With maple, Whipstitch I to A/B Assembly.

A/B Assembly

I

J

Step 2:
Starting at ♦, wrap cord around J until completely covered; secure ends of cord to stitches on wrong side of I.

Backstitch, embroider eye detail and nostrils on A pieces as indicated on graphs.

NOTE: Cut away ends of four craft or ice cream sticks to measure 3" [7.6cm] long.

3: Glue 3" sticks and two full-length sticks to wrong side of each A as indicated.

4: Whipstitch and assemble A-H pieces and cut sticks as indicated and according to Pony Assembly Diagram. For each stirrup, Whipstitch and assemble one of each I and J to each A/B assembly as indicated and according to Stirrup Assembly Diagram.

NOTE: Cut a 15" [38.1cm] length each of metallic cord and holly and red yarn.

5: For reins, braid three cut strands and glue ends under pony's chin (see photo); trim and fray ends of mane and tail strands. Glue holly leaves and pom-poms to one side of Pony (see photo); insert clock in cutout (see photo). ✿

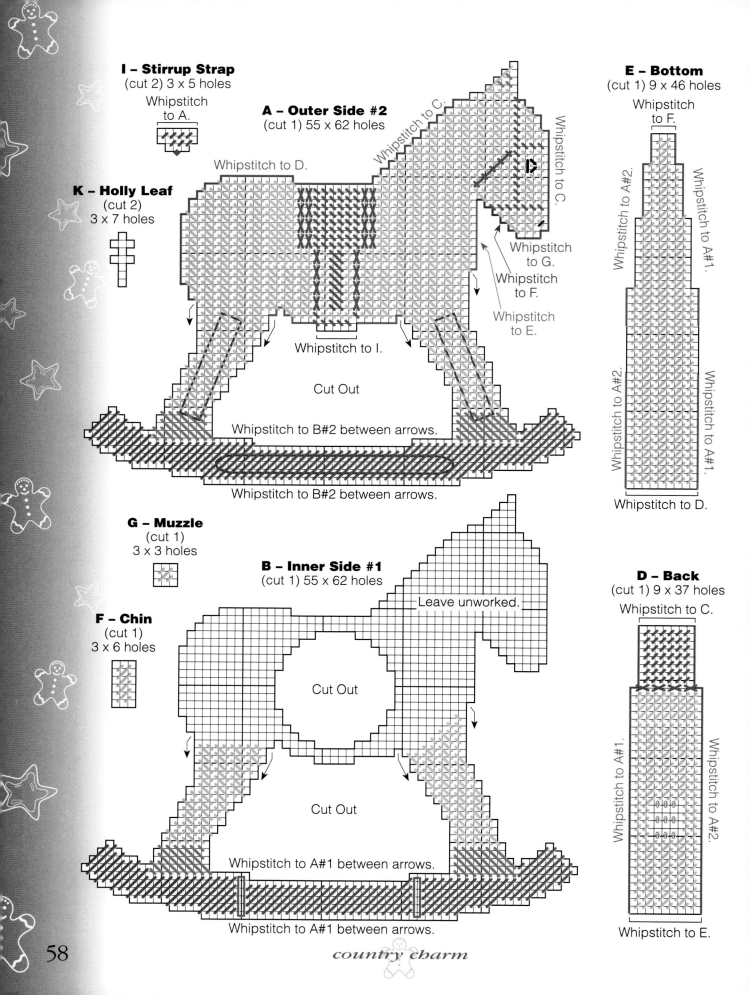

I – Stirrup Strap
(cut 2) 3 x 5 holes
Whipstitch to A.

A – Outer Side #2
(cut 1) 55 x 62 holes

Whipstitch to C.

E – Bottom
(cut 1) 9 x 46 holes
Whipstitch to F.

Whipstitch to D.

Whipstitch to C.

K – Holly Leaf
(cut 2)
3 x 7 holes

Whipstitch to G.

Whipstitch to F.

Whipstitch to E.

Whipstitch to A#2.

Whipstitch to A#1.

Whipstitch to A#2.

Whipstitch to A#1.

Whipstitch to I.

Cut Out

Whipstitch to B#2 between arrows.

Whipstitch to B#2 between arrows.

Whipstitch to D.

G – Muzzle
(cut 1)
3 x 3 holes

B – Inner Side #1
(cut 1) 55 x 62 holes

Leave unworked.

D – Back
(cut 1) 9 x 37 holes
Whipstitch to C.

F – Chin
(cut 1)
3 x 6 holes

Cut Out

Whipstitch to A#1.

Whipstitch to A#2.

Cut Out

Whipstitch to A#1 between arrows.

Whipstitch to A#1 between arrows.

Whipstitch to E.

58

B – Inner Side #2
(cut 1) 55 x 62 holes

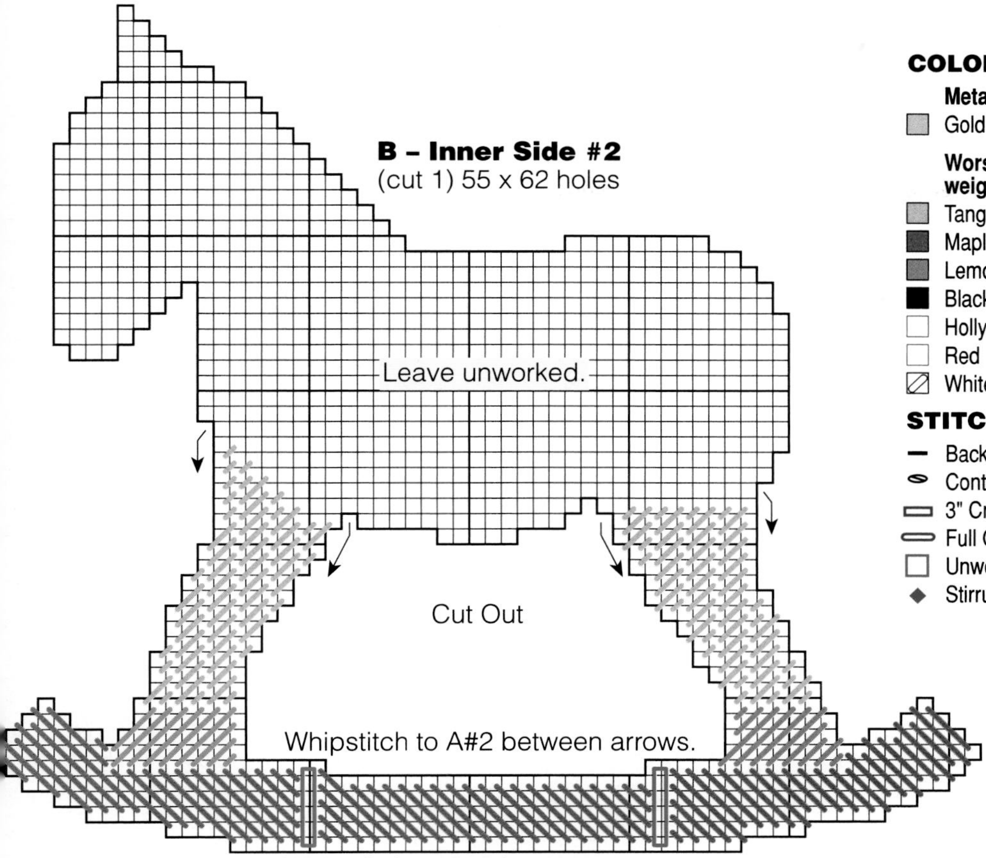

Leave unworked.

Cut Out

Whipstitch to A#2 between arrows.

Whipstitch to A#2 between arrows.

H – Brace Piece
(cut 4) 5 x 17 holes

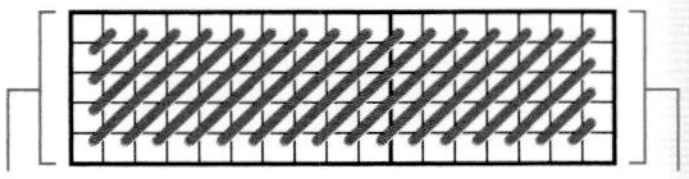

Whipstitch to one inner A piece.

C – Top
(cut 1) 7 x 44 holes

Whipstitch to G.

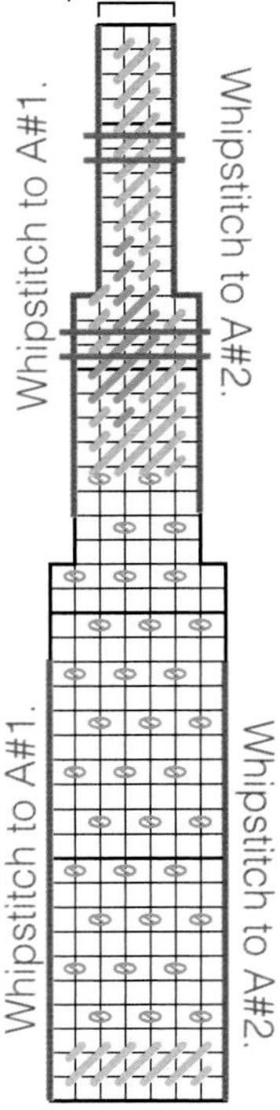

Whipstitch to A#1.

Whipstitch to A#2.

Whipstitch to A#1.

Whipstitch to A#2.

Whipstitch to D.

A – Outer Side #1
(cut 1) 55 x 62 holes

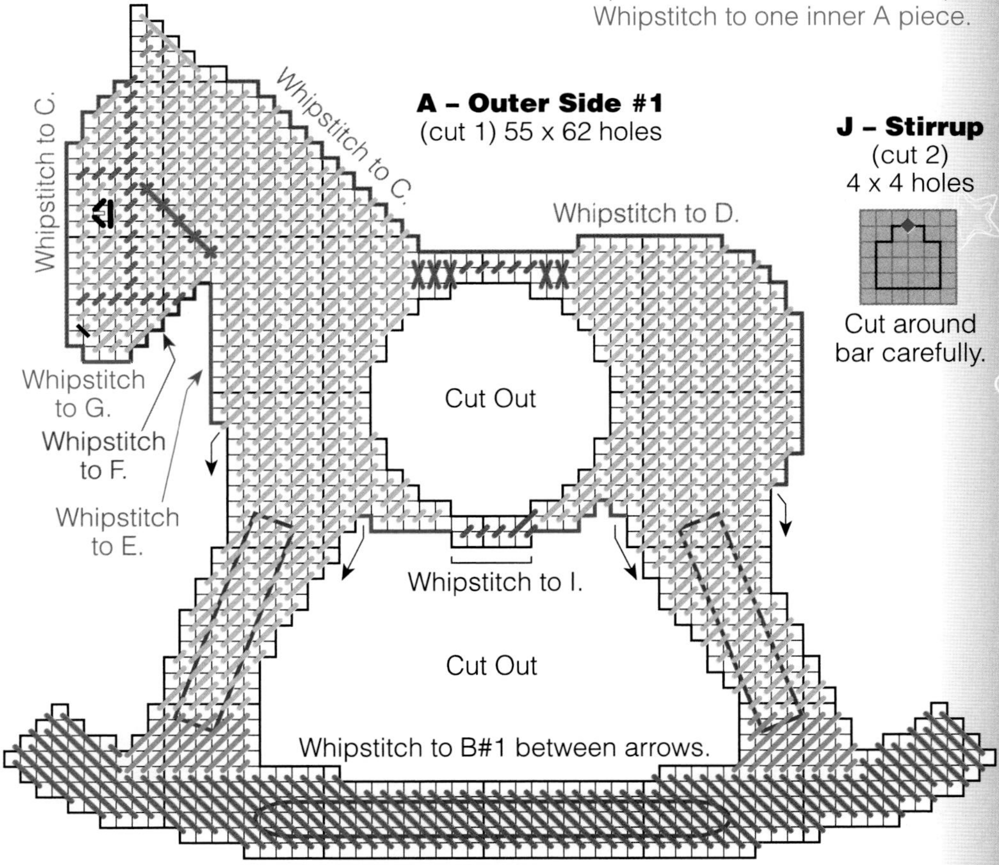

Whipstitch to C.

Whipstitch to C.

Whipstitch to D.

Cut Out

Whipstitch to G.

Whipstitch to F.

Whipstitch to E.

Whipstitch to I.

Cut Out

Whipstitch to B#1 between arrows.

Whipstitch to B#1 between arrows.

J – Stirrup
(cut 2)
4 x 4 holes

Cut around bar carefully.

designed by
Michele
Wilcox

holiday *charmer*

skill level & size

Easy skill level. 2¾" x 13" [7cm x 33cm].

materials

- One sheet of 7-count plastic canvas
- #5 perle coton or six-strand embroidery floss; for amount see Color Key.
- Worsted-weight or plastic canvas yarn; for amounts see Color Key.

cutting instructions

For Holiday Charmer, cut one according to graph on page 63.

stitching instructions

1: Using colors indicated and Continental Stitch, work according to graph; fill in uncoded areas using red and Continental Stitch. With matching colors, Overcast edges.

2: Using perle coton or three strands floss and embroidery stitches indicated, embroider detail as indicated on graph. 🍪

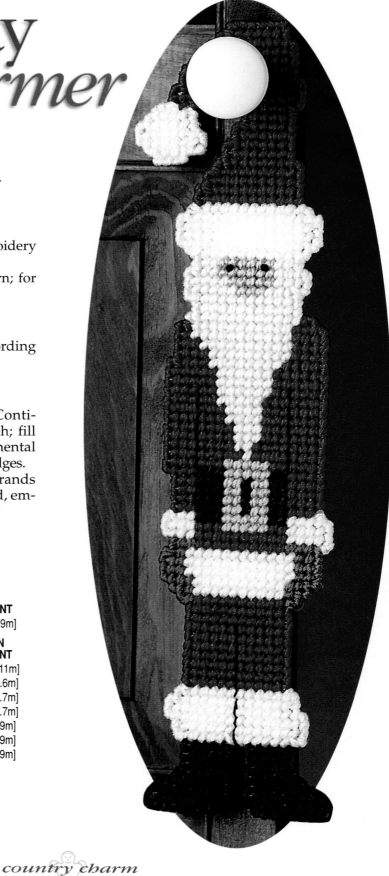

COLOR KEY: Holiday Charmer

#5 perle coton or floss		DMC®	AMOUNT
■ Black		#310	1 yd. [0.9m]

Worsted-weight	Nylon Plus™	Need-loft®	YARN AMOUNT
☐ Red	#20	#01	12 yds. [11m]
White	#01	#41	5 yds. [4.6m]
Black	#02	#00	3 yds. [2.7m]
▨ Eggshell	#24	#39	3 yds. [2.7m]
Coral	#14	–	1 yd. [0.9m]
Holly	#31	#27	1 yd. [0.9m]
Tangerine	#15	#11	1 yd. [0.9m]

STITCH KEY:
- — Backstitch/Straight
- • French Knot

birdhouse gift box

designed by
Jaimie
Davenport

skill level & size

Average skill level. 4¼" x 5" x 6" tall [10.8cm x 12.7cm x 15.2cm].

materials

- One sheet of 7-count plastic canvas
- 9" [22.9cm] length of ⅛" [3mm] red satin ribbon
- One ⅜" [10mm] white shank button
- Sewing needle and brown thread
- Worsted-weight or plastic canvas yarn; for amounts see Color Key on page 62.

cutting instructions

A: For front and back, cut one each according to graphs.
B: For sides cut two 22 x 25 holes.
C: For roof pieces, cut two 22 x 25 holes.
D: For eave #1 pieces, cut four 2 x 25 holes (no graph).

E: For eave #2 pieces, cut two 4 x 25 holes (no graph).

F: For bottom, cut one 19 x 25 holes (no graph).

stitching instructions

NOTE: F piece is not worked.

1: Using colors and stitches indicated, work A-C pieces according to graphs; using cinnamon and Continental Stitch, work D and E pieces.

2: Whipstitch A-F pieces together according to Birdhouse Assembly Diagram; with cinnamon, overcast unfinished edges.

3: Assemble button and ribbon on roof pieces according to Closure Assembly Diagram.

A – Front
(cut 1) 31 x 37 holes

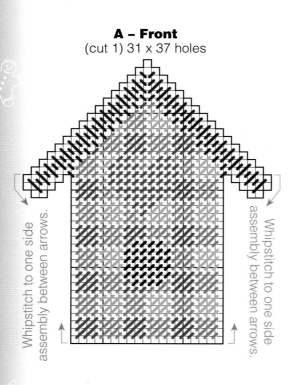

Whipstitch to one side assembly between arrows.

Whipstitch to one side assembly between arrows.

COLOR KEY: Birdhouse Gift Box

	Worsted-weight	Nylon Plus™	Need-loft®	YARN AMOUNT
■	Cinnamon	#44	#14	20 yds. [18.3m]
■	Holly	#31	#27	18 yds. [16.5m]
■	Moss	#48	#25	15 yds. [13.7m]
■	White	#01	#41	12 yds. [11m]
■	Black	#02	#00	1 yd. [0.9m]
■	Red	#20	#01	1 yd. [0.9m]

B – Side
(cut 2) 22 x 25 holes

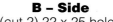

Birdhouse Assembly Diagram

(Pieces are shown in different colors for contrast; gray denotes wrong side.)

Step 1:
For each side assembly (make 2), with cinnamon, Whipstitch one B, two D and one E wrong sides together.

Step 3:
Whipstitch one C to each side assembly (**NOTE:** One C shown in outline form for clarity.).

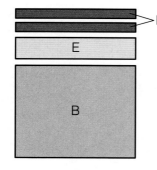

D

E

B

Step 2:
With cinnamon for roof area and with holly, Whipstitch side assemblies, A and F pieces together.

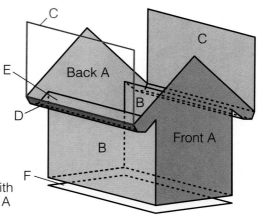

C

Back A

E

D

B

Front A

B

F

A – Back
(cut 1) 31 x 37 holes
Overcast between arrows.

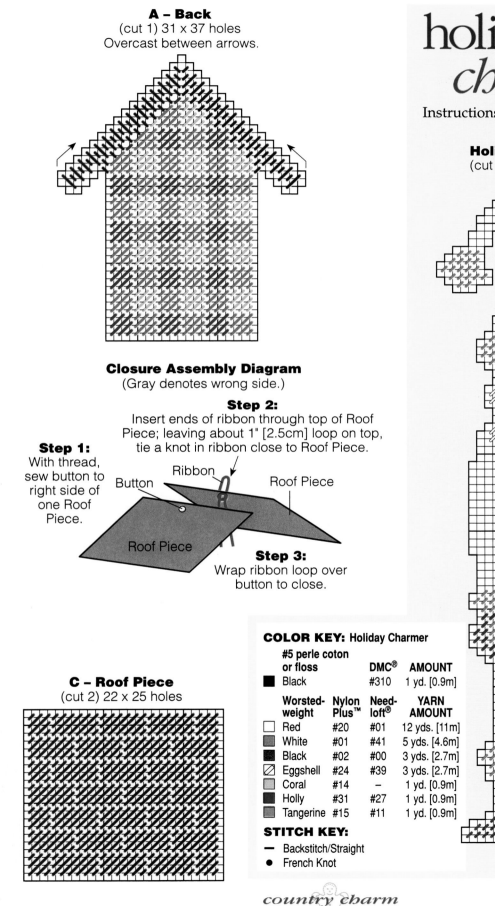

holiday
charmer
Instructions & photo on page 60

Holiday Charmer
(cut 1) 23 x 86 holes

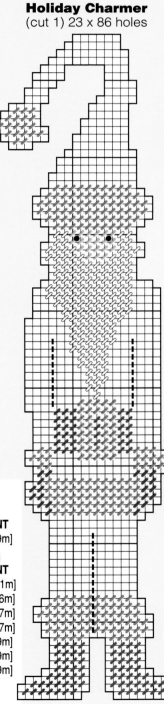

Closure Assembly Diagram
(Gray denotes wrong side.)

Step 1:
With thread, sew button to right side of one Roof Piece.

Step 2:
Insert ends of ribbon through top of Roof Piece; leaving about 1" [2.5cm] loop on top, tie a knot in ribbon close to Roof Piece.

Ribbon

Button

Roof Piece

Roof Piece

Step 3:
Wrap ribbon loop over button to close.

C – Roof Piece
(cut 2) 22 x 25 holes

COLOR KEY: Holiday Charmer

#5 perle coton or floss		DMC®	AMOUNT
■ Black		#310	1 yd. [0.9m]

	Worsted-weight	Nylon Plus™	Need-loft®	YARN AMOUNT
☐	Red	#20	#01	12 yds. [11m]
▨	White	#01	#41	5 yds. [4.6m]
■	Black	#02	#00	3 yds. [2.7m]
▨	Eggshell	#24	#39	3 yds. [2.7m]
▨	Coral	#14	–	1 yd. [0.9m]
■	Holly	#31	#27	1 yd. [0.9m]
▨	Tangerine	#15	#11	1 yd. [0.9m]

STITCH KEY:
– Backstitch/Straight
• French Knot

designed by
Michele Wilcox

winter *wonderland*

skill level & size

Easy skill level. 10" x 10½" [25.4cm x 26.7cm].

materials

- One sheet of 7-count plastic canvas
- One 9" x 12" [22.9cm x 30.5cm] sheet of white adhesive-backed felt
- Pastel crystal glitter paint
- ⅔-yd. [0.6m] length of white ¼" [6mm] satin ribbon
- #3 and #5 perle coton or six-strand embroidery floss; for amounts see Color Key.
- Worsted-weight or plastic canvas yarn; for amounts see Color Key.

cutting instructions

For Winter Wonderland, cut one according to graph.

stitching instructions

1: Using colors and stitches indicated, work according to graph; fill in uncoded areas using denim and Continental Stitch. With red, Overcast edges.

2: Using perle coton or floss in colors and embroidery stitches indicated, embroider detail as indicated on graph.

NOTE: For backing, using canvas piece as a pattern, cut one from felt ⅛" [3mm] smaller at all edges.

3: For hanger, thread ends of ribbon from back to front through ◆ hole as indicated on graph; tie ribbon ends into a bow. Adhere felt backing to wrong side of piece.

4: Apply glitter paint to trees and ground (see photo) for a snow effect.

COLOR KEY: Winter Wonderland

#3 perle coton or six-strand floss	DMC®	AMOUNT
■ Black	White	2 yds. [1.8m]
■ White	#310	2 yds. [1.8m]

#5 perle coton or three-strand floss	DMC®	AMOUNT
■ Black	#310	4 yds. [3.7m]
■ Lemon	#307	¼ yd. [0.2m]

Worsted-weight	Nylon Plus™	Need-loft®	YARN AMOUNT
☐ Denim	#06	–	35 yds. [32m]
■ White	#01	#41	30 yds. [27.4m]

Worsted-weight	Nylon Plus™	Need-loft®	YARN AMOUNT
■ Fern	#57	#23	8 yds. [7.3m]
■ Lavender	#12	#05	6 yds. [5.5m]
■ Mint	#30	–	6 yds. [5.5m]
■ Red	#20	#01	6 yds. [5.5m]
☐ Tangerine	#15	#11	6 yds. [5.5m]
■ Camel	#34	#43	4 yds. [3.7m]
■ Royal	#09	#32	4 yds. [3.7m]
■ Black	#02	#00	3 yds. [2.7m]
■ Cinnamon	#44	#14	3 yds. [2.7m]
☐ Coral	#14	–	1 yd. [0.9m]
▨ Yellow	#26	#57	1 yd. [0.9m]

STITCH KEY:
— Backstitch/Straight
● French Knot
◆ Hanger Attachment

 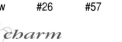

designed by
Michele Wilcox

joy to the world stocking

skill level & size

Easy skill level. 9" x 11½" [22.9cm x 29.2cm].

materials

- Two sheets of 7-count plastic canvas
- One ¾" [19mm] yellow star button
- Two gold ½" [13mm] jingle bells
- ⅓ yd. [0.3m] green ¼" [6mm] satin ribbon
- #3 and #5 perle coton or six-strand embroidery floss, for amounts see Color Key.
- Worsted-weight or plastic canvas yarn, for amounts see Color Key.

cutting instructions

For Stocking front and back, cut two (one for front and one for back) according to graph.

stitching instructions

1: Using colors indicated and Continental Stitch, work one piece for front according to graph; work remaining piece on opposite side of canvas for back according to Back Stitch Pattern Guide. Fill in uncoded areas of front A using teal blue and Continental Stitch.

2: Using perle coton or floss in colors and embroidery stitches indicated, embroider detail on front as indicated on graph; sew button to front at ◆ hole as indicated.

3: With red yarn,

Whipstitch pieces wrong sides together as indicated; Overcast unfinished top edges.

4: For hanger, fold ribbon in half and tie into

Stocking Front & Back
(cut 1 each) 58 x 77 holes

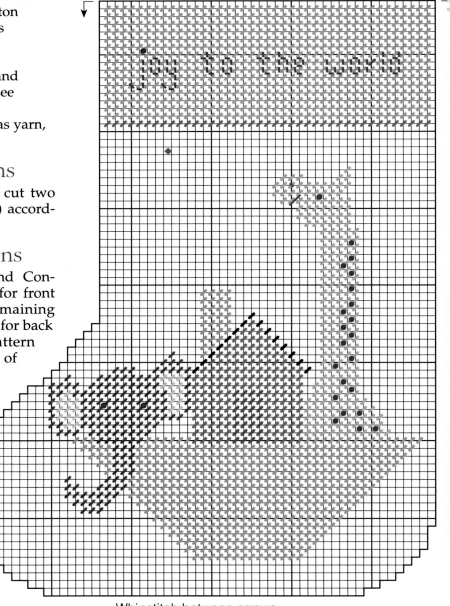

Whipstitch between arrows.

a knot half way down ribbon; thread ends through holes in top right corner of stocking (see photo); tie ends into a knot close to Stocking. Tie bells on each end of ribbon. 🎄

COLOR KEY: Joy To The World Stocking

#3 perle coton or six-strand floss	DMC®	AMOUNT
Light Brown	#434	2 yds. [1.8m]
Red	#321	2 yds. [1.8m]

#5 perle coton or three-strand floss	DMC®	AMOUNT
Black	#310	1 yd. [0.9m]

Worsted-weight	Nylon Plus™	Need-loft®	YARN AMOUNT
Teal Blue	#08	–	85 yds. [77.7m]
Eggshell	#24	#39	12 yds. [11m]
Maple	#35	#13	10 yds. [9.1m]
Tangerine	#15	#11	5 yds. [4.6m]
Pewter	#40	–	4 yds. [3.7m]
Red	#20	#01	4 yds. [3.7m]
Black	#02	#00	1 yd. [0.9m]
Camel	#34	#43	1 yd. [0.9m]
Coral	#14	–	1 yd. [0.9m]
Holly	#31	#27	1 yd. [0.9m]

STITCH KEY:

— Backstitch/Straight

● French Knot

◆ Star Button Attachment

↑ Continue established pattern across entire piece. ↑

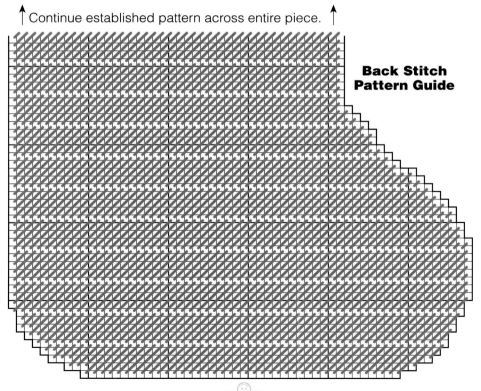

Back Stitch Pattern Guide

designed by
Susan
Leinberger

handy *helpers*
winter warmers

skill level & size

Average skill level. Each is 5" x 5¼" [12.7cm x 13.3cm], not including clothespin.

materials

- One sheet of 7-count plastic canvas
- One 9" x 12" [22.9cm x 30.5cm] sheet of adhesive-backed burgundy felt
- Two spring-type clothespins

- Craft glue or glue gun
- #3 perle coton or six-strand embroidery floss; for amounts see Color Key.
- Worsted-weight or plastic canvas yarn; for amounts see Color Key.

cutting instructions

A: For mitten minder, cut one 32 x 35 holes.
B: For hat holder, cut one 32 x 35 holes.
C: For clip covers, cut two 3 x 22 holes.

stitching instructions

1: Using colors and stitches indicated, work A, B (leave ¼" loops on Modified Turkey Work Stitch) and C (substitute ultra dk. pistachio green for buff and gold for burgundy on one C piece) pieces according to graphs.

2: With matching colors as shown in photo, Overcast edges.

3: Using perle coton or six strands floss and yarn (Separate into individual plies, if desired) in colors and embroidery stitches indicated, embroider detail on A and B pieces as indicated on graphs.

NOTE: For backings, using A and B pieces as patterns, cut one each from felt ⅛" [3mm] smaller at all edges.

4: Adhere one backing to wrong side of each A and B; glue one C to one side of each clothespin (see photo). Glue opposite side of each clothespin to matching A or B as shown in photo. ✿

COLOR KEY: Handy Helpers

#3 perle coton or floss	DMC®	AMOUNT
■ Topaz	#725	2 yds. [1.8m]
■ Ultra Dk. Pistachio Green	#890	2 yds. [1.8m]

Worsted-weight	Red Heart®	YARN AMOUNT
■ Soft Navy	#387	16 yds. [14.6m]
■ Buff	#334	14 yds. [12.8m]
■ Burgundy	#376	10 yds. [9.1m]
■ Hunter Green	#389	8 yds. [7.3m]
■ Gold	#321	3 yds. [2.7m]
■ White	#311	2 yds. [1.8m]

STITCH KEY:

- — Backstitch/Straight
- • French Knot
- ∾ Modified Turkey Work

C – Clip Cover
(cut 2)
3 x 22 holes

A – Mitten Minder
(cut 1) 32 x 35 holes

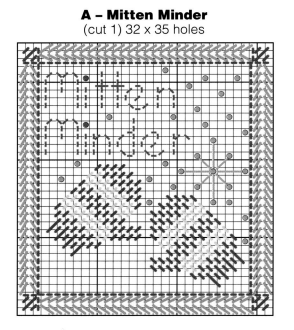

B – Hat Holder
(cut 1) 32 x 35 holes

country charm

gingerbread boy & girl

designed by **Candy Clayton**

skill level & size

Average skill level. Gingerbread Girl is 13" x 18¾" [33cm x 47.6cm]; Gingerbread Boy is 13" x 18" [33cm x 45.7cm].

materials

- Four 13½" x 22½" [34.3cm x 57.2cm] sheets of 7-count plastic canvas
- Craft glue or glue gun
- Heavy metallic braid or metallic cord; for amount see Color Key.
- Worsted-weight or plastic canvas yarn; for amounts see Color Key.

cutting instructions

A: For Gingerbread Girl front and backing, cut two (one for front and one for backing) according to graph.

B: For Gingerbread Girl bow front and backing, cut two (one for front and one for backing) according to graph.

C: For Gingerbread Boy front and backing, cut two (one for front and one for backing) according to graph.

D: For Gingerbread Boy bow front and backing, cut two (one for front and one for backing) according to graph.

E: For buttons, cut two according to graph.

stitching instructions

NOTE: One of each A-D pieces are not worked for backings.

1: Using colors and stitches indicated, work one of each A-D for fronts and E piece according to graphs; fill in uncoded areas on front A and C using maple and Continental Stitch. With matching color, Overcast edges of E pieces.

2: Using braid or cord and yarn (Separate into individual plies, if desired.) in colors and embroidery stitches indicated, embroider detail on A and C pieces as indicated on graphs.

3: Holding one backing to wrong side of each corresponding front, with forest for girl bow and with matching colors, Whipstitch together.

4: Glue wrong side of one bow and buttons to right side of each corresponding Gingerbread Boy or Girl as shown in photo.

D – Gingerbread Boy Bow Front & Backing
(cut 1 each) 11 x 18 holes

COLOR KEY: Gingerbread Boy & Girl

	Heavy metallic braid or cord			AMOUNT
▨	Gold			3 yds. [2.7m]

	Worsted-weight	Nylon Plus™	Need-loft®	YARN AMOUNT
▨	Holly	#31	#27	60 yds. [54.9m]
□	Maple	#35	#13	55 yds. [50.3m]
▨	Xmas Red	#19	#02	45 yds. [41.1m]
▨	Forest	#32	#29	25 yds. [22.9m]
▨	Red	#20	#01	25 yds. [22.9m]
▨	White	#01	#41	10 yds. [9.1m]
■	Black	#02	#00	6 yds. [5.5m]
▨	Pink	#11	#07	5 yds. [4.6m]

STITCH KEY:
- — Backstitch/Straight
- ● French Knot
- ✱ Smyrna Cross
- ⟳ Lazy Daisy
- ◆ Button Placement

B – Gingerbread Girl Bow Front & Backing
(cut 1 each) 10 x 22 holes

E – Button
(cut 2) 4 x 4 holes

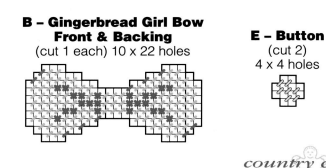

**A – Gingerbread Girl
Front & Backing**
(cut 1 each)
87 x 116 holes

COLOR KEY:
Heavy metallic braid or cord
⬛ Gold

Worsted-weight
⬛ Holly
⬜ Maple
⬜ Xmas Red
⬛ Forest
⬛ Red
⬜ White
⬛ Black
⬛ Pink

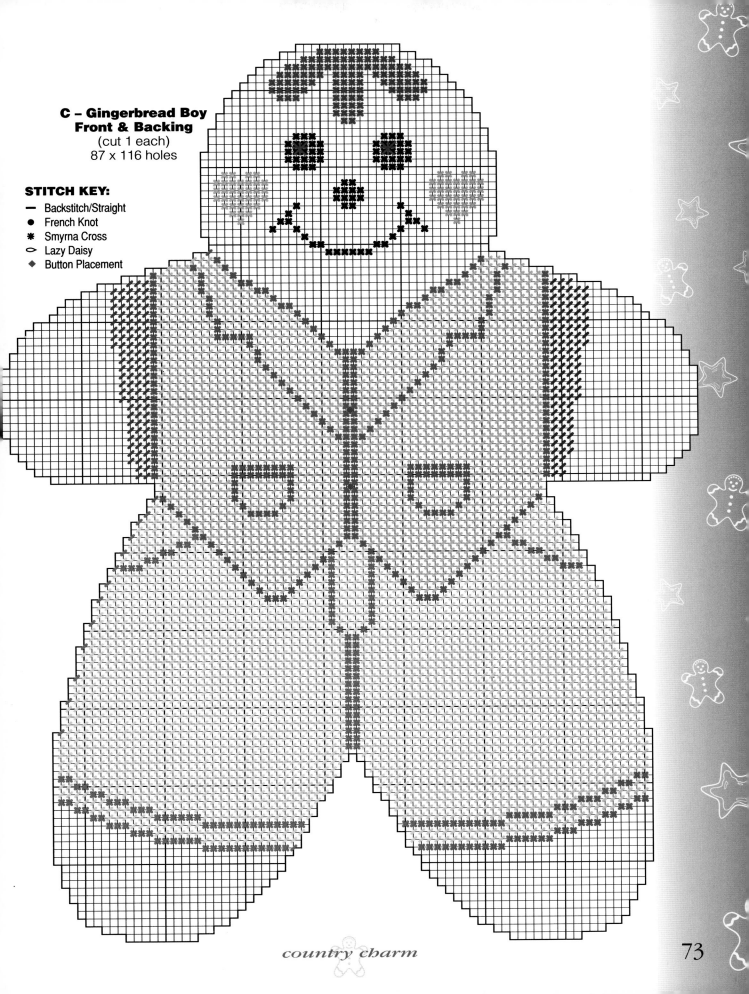

**C – Gingerbread Boy
Front & Backing**
(cut 1 each)
87 x 116 holes

STITCH KEY:
— Backstitch/Straight
● French Knot
✳ Smyrna Cross
◠ Lazy Daisy
◆ Button Placement

country charm

designed by
**Sandra
Miller Maxfield**

holiday *utensil holder*

skill level & size

Average skill level. Each is 4¾" x 8¼" [12.1cm x 21cm].

materials for four

- Two sheets of 7-count plastic canvas
- Craft glue or glue gun
- Worsted-weight or plastic canvas yarn; for amounts see Color Key.

cutting instructions

A: For backs, cut four according to graph.
B: For hats, cut four according to graph.
C: For faces, cut four according to graph.
D: For mustaches, cut four according to graph.
E: For eyebrows, cut eight according to graph.

stitching instructions

1: Using colors and stitches indicated, work A-D according to graphs; with white for E pieces and with matching colors, Overcast edges of D, E and indicated edges of B and C pieces.

2: Using black (Separate into individual plies, if desired.) and Backstitch, embroider eyelashes on C as indicated on graph.

3: For each Holder (make 4), holding wrong side of one B and one C to right side of one A, with cherry red for hat and white for face, Whipstitch together.

4: Glue wrong side of one D to right side of each C as indicated. Display as desired.

COLOR KEY: Holiday Utensil Holder

	Worsted-weight	Red Heart®	YARN AMOUNT
▨	White	#1	56 yds. [51.2m]
■	Cherry Red	#912	21 yds. [19.2m]
▦	Tan	#334	21 yds. [19.2m]
▨	Pale Rose	#755	2 yds. [1.8m]
■	Black	#12	1 yd. [0.9m]

STITCH KEY:

─	Backstitch/Straight	☐ Face Attachment
☐	Hat Attachment	☐ Mustache Attachment

A – Back
(cut 4) 28 x 55 holes

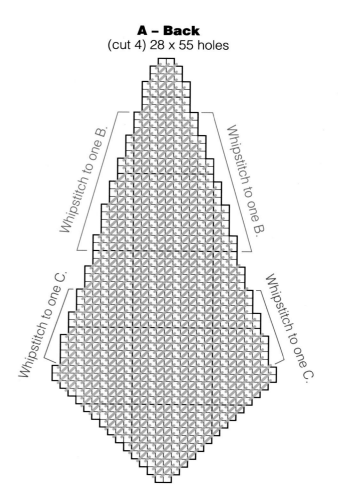

B – Hat
(cut 4) 18 x 18 holes

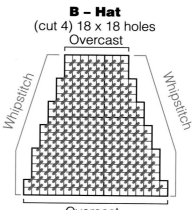

D – Mustache
(cut 4) 8 x 30 holes

E – Eyebrow
(cut 8)
3 x 5 holes

C – Face
(cut 4) 10 x 26 holes
Overcast

Whipstitch

Whipstitch

Overcast

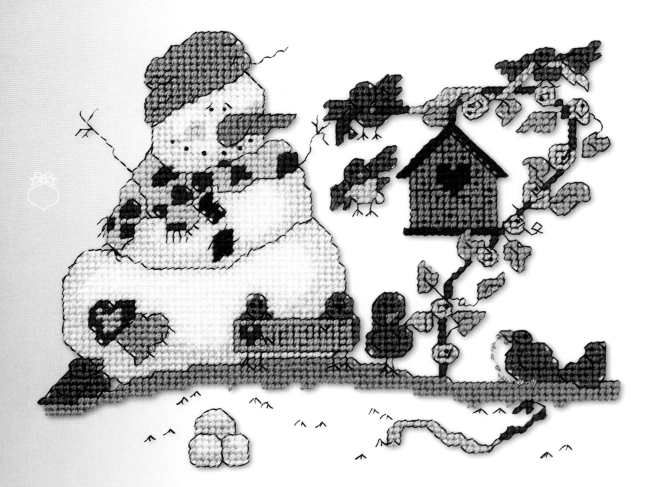

Our snow fellow joins his bird friends to guide us through a more traditional touch of Christmas. But tradition doesn't mean boring! If you look close you'll see Santa and his sweetie sneaking a kiss under the mistletoe and a sweet treat for all in the Christmas countdown.

yuletide
traditions

designed by
Christine A. Hendricks

birdseed snowman

skill level & size

Average skill level. 13¼" x 17¾" tall [33.7cm x 45.1cm].

materials

- One 13½" x 22½" [34.3cm x 57.2cm] sheet of 7-count plastic canvas
- #12 Tapestry braid or metallic cord; for amount see Color Key.
- Six-strand embroidery floss; for amount see Color Key.
- Worsted-weight or plastic canvas yarn; for amounts see Color Key.

cutting instructions

For Birdseed Snowman, cut one 88 x 118 holes.

stitching instructions

1: Using colors and stitches indicated, work according to graph; fill in uncoded areas using white and Continental Stitch. With white, Overcast edges.

2: Using three strands floss and braid in colors and embroidery stitches indicated, embroider detail as indicated on graph.

3: Hang or display as desired.

COLOR KEY: Birdseed Snowman

Metallic braid or cord	Kreinik Tapestry™		AMOUNT
Gold	#002		1 yd. [0.9m]

Embroidery floss	DMC®		AMOUNT
Black	#310		20 yds. [18.3m]

Worsted-weight	Nylon Plus™	Need-loft®	YARN AMOUNT
White	#01	#41	3 oz. [85.1g]
Denim	#06	–	10 yds. [9.1m]
Flesh Tone	–	#56	8 yds. [7.3m]
Sail Blue	#04	#35	8 yds. [7.3m]
Burgundy	#13	#03	6 yds. [5.5m]
Pink	#11	#07	6 yds. [5.5m]
Fern	#57	#23	5 yds. [4.6m]
Sandstone	#47	#16	4 yds. [3.7m]
Yellow	#26	#57	4 yds. [3.7m]
Gray	#23	#38	3 yds. [2.7m]
Lavender	#12	#05	3 yds. [2.7m]
Pumpkin	#50	#12	3 yds. [2.7m]
Silver	–	#37	3 yds. [2.7m]
Black	#02	#00	2 yds. [1.8m]
Camel	#34	#43	2 yds. [1.8m]

STITCH KEY:

- — Backstitch/Straight
- ● French Knot

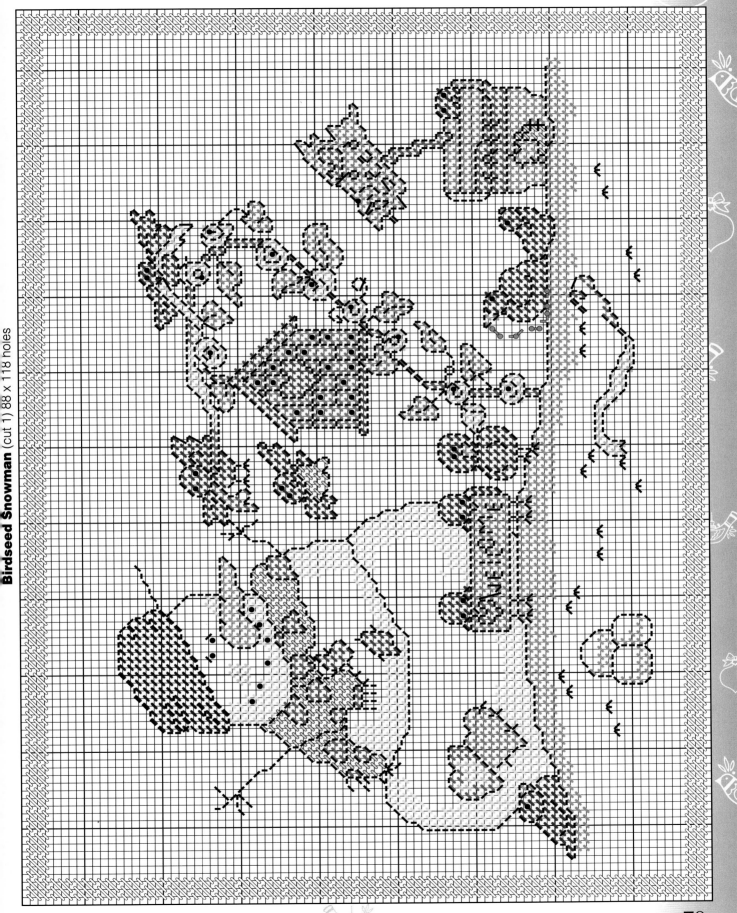

Birdseed Snowman (cut 1) 88 x 118 holes

victorian ornaments

designed by
Mary Layfield

skill level & sizes

Challenging skill level. Boot is 3¼" x 5" [8.3cm x 12.7cm]; Diamond is 3¼" x 4⅜" [8.3cm x 11.1cm]; Teardrop is 3" x 5½" [7.6cm x 14cm]; Heart is 4⅜" x 4½" [11.1cm x 11.4cm]; Fan is 4" x 5⅞" [10.2cm x 14.9cm]; Bell is 3¾" x 4⅜" [9.5cm x 11.1cm]. Measurements do not include lace or hangers.

materials

- Two sheets of 7-count plastic canvas
- 66 white 2½mm and 26 white 4mm round pearl beads
- Beading needle and thread
- Two light pink marabou feathers
- 1½ yds. [1.4m] of ecru ½" [13mm] pregathered lace
- Craft glue or glue gun
- Six-strand embroidery floss; for amount see Color Key.
- Worsted-weight or plastic canvas yarn; for amounts see Color Key.

cutting instructions

For Ornament fronts and backings, cut two each (one each for front and one each for backing) according to graphs.

stitching instructions

NOTE: One of each Ornament is not worked for backing.

1: Using colors and stitches indicated, work one of each Ornament for front according to graphs.

2: Using six strands floss and yarn in colors and embroidery stitches indicated, embroider detail on each front as indicated on graphs; using eggshell and Modified Turkey Work Stitch (leave 1" [2.5cm] loop), embroider Boot lace loop through ◆ hole as indicated. Working from back to front, pull 2" [5.1cm] of eggshell yarn through ★ hole as indicated, forming Boot lace string; knot end to prevent fraying and trim close to knot.

3: Using beading needle and thread, sew 4mm beads to Boot, Diamond, and Bell fronts

---

**Diamond Ornament
Front & Backing**
(cut 1 each)
21 x 29 holes

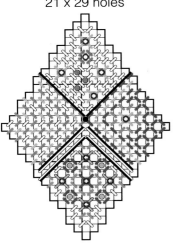

STITCH KEY:
- — Backstitch/Straight
- ● French Knot
- ○ Bead Attachment
- ◇ Boot Lace Loop
- ★ Boot Lace String
- ▲ Pearl Loop

COLOR KEY: Victorian Ornaments

Embroidery floss			AMOUNT
■ Black			10 yds. [9.1m]

	Worsted-weight	Nylon Plus™	Need-loft®	YARN AMOUNT
▨	Eggshell	#24	#39	24 yds. [21.9m]
▨	Baby Blue	#05	#36	16 yds. [14.6m]
▨	Moss	#48	#25	16 yds. [14.6m]
▨	Pink	#11	#07	16 yds. [14.6m]
▨	Sail Blue	#04	#35	16 yds. [14.6m]
▨	Lavender	#12	#05	12 yds. [11m]

**Boot Ornament
Front & Backing**
(cut 1 each) 22 x 32 holes

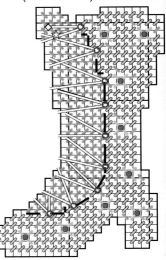

and 2½mm beads to Fan front as indicated. For each pearl loop (make 4), string fourteen 2½mm beads onto thread; sew two pearl loops to each ▲ hole on Heart and Fan as indicated, forming bows.

4: With eggshell for top edges of Boot and with matching colors as shown in photo, Whipstitch corresponding backing to wrong side of each Boot and Bell front; with pink for pink edge of Fan (see photo) and with eggshell, Whipstitch corresponding backing to wrong side of each Teardrop, Diamond, Fan and Heart front.

NOTE: Cut one 3" [7.6cm], one 9" [22.9cm], one 12" [30.5cm] and two 15" [38.1cm] lengths of lace.

5: Trimming away excess as needed to fit, glue 3" lace to top edge of Boot and 9" lace to top edge of Fan; glue 12" lace around edges of Diamond and one 15" lace around edges of each Teardrop and Heart. Glue feathers to Teardrop and Fan as shown.

6: Hang or display as desired.

STITCH KEY:
- — Backstitch/Straight
- ● French Knot
- ○ Bead Attachment
- ◇ Boot Lace Loop
- ★ Boot Lace String
- ▲ Pearl Loop

COLOR KEY: Victorian Ornaments

Embroidery floss			AMOUNT
■ Black			10 yds. [9.1m]

Worsted-weight	Nylon Plus™	Needloft®	YARN AMOUNT
▨ Eggshell	#24	#39	24 yds. [21.9m]
▨ Baby Blue	#05	#36	16 yds. [14.6m]
▨ Moss	#48	#25	16 yds. [14.6m]
▨ Pink	#11	#07	16 yds. [14.6m]
▨ Sail Blue	#04	#35	16 yds. [14.6m]
▨ Lavender	#12	#05	12 yds. [11m]

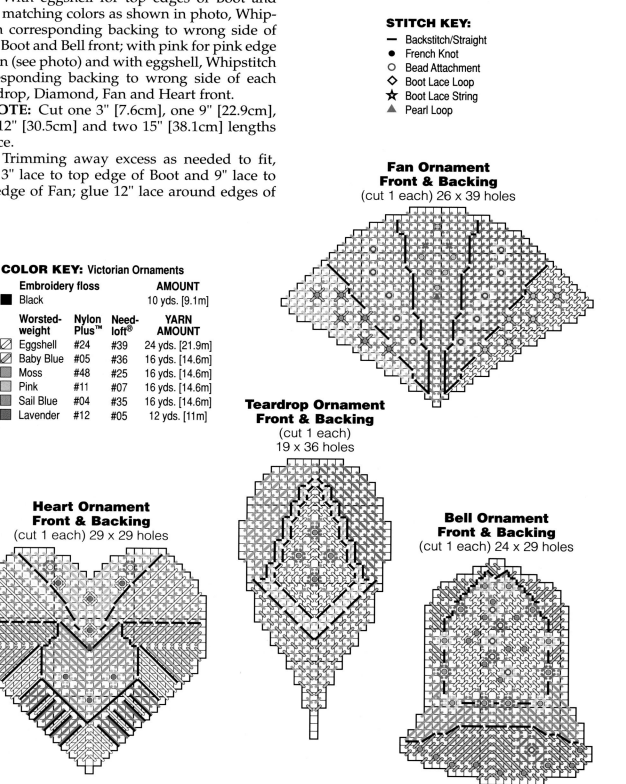

Fan Ornament Front & Backing
(cut 1 each) 26 x 39 holes

Teardrop Ornament Front & Backing
(cut 1 each) 19 x 36 holes

Heart Ornament Front & Backing
(cut 1 each) 29 x 29 holes

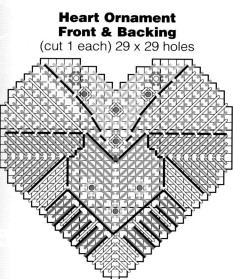

Bell Ornament Front & Backing
(cut 1 each) 24 x 29 holes

christmas
in your
heart

designed by
Janelle Giese of
Janelle Marie
Designs

christmas in your *heart*

skill level & size

Challenging skill level. 6¼" x 11¼" tall [15.9cm x 28.6cm].

materials

- One sheet of 7-count plastic canvas
- Two Darice® 3" [7.6cm] plastic canvas circles
- 4½" [11.4cm] length of ¼" [6mm] wooden dowel
- One 1¾" [4.4cm] wooden wheel
- White craft paint and paintbrush
- Aquarium gravel or other weighting material
- Craft glue or glue gun
- #8 perle coton or six-strand embroidery floss; for amount see Color Key.
- ⅛" [3mm] metallic ribbon or metallic cord; for amounts see Color Key.
- Chenille yarn; for amount see Color Key.
- Worsted-weight or plastic canvas yarn; for amounts see Color Key.

cutting instructions

A: For motif, cut one according to graph.
B: For base side, cut one 8 x 67 holes.
C: For base top, cut one from one circle according to graph.
D: For base bottom, use remaining circle (no graph).

stitching instructions

NOTE: D is not worked.
1: Using colors and stitches indicated, work A, B (overlap ends as indicated on graph and work through both thicknesses at overlap area to join) and C pieces according to graphs.

2: With gold for heart and with matching colors as shown in photo, Overcast edges of A and cutout edges of C.

3: Using perle coton or two strands floss and ribbon or cord in colors and embroidery stitches indicated, embroider detail on A and B pieces as indicated.

NOTE: Cut two 9" [22.9cm] lengths of ribbon or cord.

4: Tie each length into a bow; trim ends. Glue one bow to each gift as shown in photo.

5: Glue one end of dowel inside center opening of wheel; paint dowel and let dry. Push opposite end of dowel through cutout on C. With Xmas green, Whipstitch B-D pieces together, filling with gravel before closing (see Base Assembly Illustration).

6: Glue motif to dowel as shown.

Base Assembly Illustration

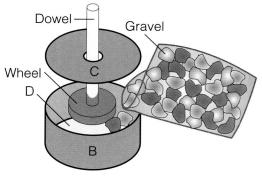

Dowel — Gravel — Wheel D — C — B

B – Base Side (cut 1) 8 x 67 holes

Lap Over — Lap Under

A – Motif
(cut 1) 41 x 59 holes

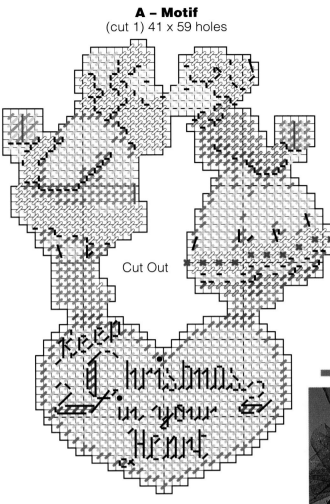

Cut Out

C – Base Top
(cut 1 from circle)
Cut out gray area.

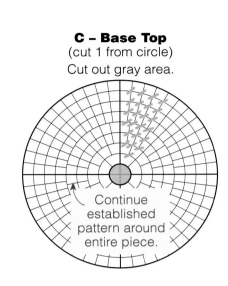

Continue established pattern around entire piece.

COLOR KEY: Christmas in Your Heart

#8 perle coton or floss	DMC®	AMOUNT
■ Black	#310	12 yds. [11m]

⅛" metallic ribbon or cord	Kreinik	AMOUNT
■ Gold	#002	5 yds. [4.6m]
■ Green	#008	4 yds. [3.7m]

Chenille yarn	Lion Brand®	YARN AMOUNT
▨ White	#100	8 yds. [7.3m]

Worsted-weight	Nylon Plus™	Need-loft®	YARN AMOUNT
▨ Xmas Red	#19	#02	18 yds. [16.5m]
▨ White	#01	#41	12 yds. [11m]
▨ Red	#20	#01	8 yds. [7.3m]
▨ Black	#02	#00	4 yds. [3.7m]
□ Xmas Green	#58	#28	4 yds. [3.7m]
▨ Flesh Tone	–	#56	3 yds. [2.7m]
■ Beige	#43	#40	2 yds. [1.8m]
▨ Eggshell	#24	#39	2 yds. [1.8m]

STITCH KEY:

— Backstitch/Straight
● French Knot

Holiday Tips

Here's a gorgeous idea! Surround a gold-wrapped box in a puff of glittery tulle, and tie with a satin bow.

Festive & Fun Gift Wrap

Materials:

Box wrapped in gold metallic paper
Black tulle with green, gold and blue sparkles
¾ yd. (0.7m) 1" (2.5cm) blue satin ribbon

Instructions:

Place box in center of tulle rectangle. Pull tulle up, smoothing up sides of box, and gather at center top. If tulle projects more than 6-8" (15.2-20.3cm) from top of box, lay flat and trim as needed. Gather at center and tie with ribbon. Trim ribbon ends in inverted V.

designed by
Janelle Giese of
Janelle Marie
Designs

santa's christmas shoppe

skill level & size

Challenging skill level. 1" x 9⅜" x 12⅛" [2.5cm x 23.8cm x 30.8cm].

materials

- ½ sheet of white and two sheets of clear 7-count plastic canvas
- One electronic music button with lights
- Craft glue or glue gun
- #5 perle coton; for amount see Color Key on page 89.
- Six-strand embroidery floss; for amount see Color Key.
- Worsted-weight or plastic canvas yarn; for amounts see Color Key.

cutting instructions

NOTE: Use white for I and clear canvas for remaining pieces.

A: For house, cut one according to graph.

B: For house roof front, cut one according to graph.

C: For house roof sides, cut two from clear 4 x 41 holes (no graph).

D: For door, cut one according to graph.

E: For door sides, cut two from clear 2 x 39 holes (no graph).

F: For door bottom, cut one from clear 2 x 20 holes (no graph).

G: For door awning front, cut one according to graph.

H: For door awning sides, cut two from clear 4 x 15 holes (no graph).

I: For exterior window, cut one according to graph.

J: For window sides #1 and #2, cut one each according to graphs.

K: For window bottom, cut one from clear 4 x 24 holes (no graph).

L: For window awning, cut one according to graph.

M: For interior window back, cut one 20 x 20 holes.

N: For interior window sides, cut four from clear 3 x 20 holes (no graph).

O: For doll, cut one according to graph.

P: For cake, cut one according to graph.

Q: For music button cover front, cut one according to graph.

R: For music button cover back, cut one from clear 10 x 10 holes (no graph).

S: For music button cover sides, cut four from clear 4 x 10 holes (no graph).

stitching instructions

NOTE: F, K and Q-S pieces are not worked.

1: Leaving uncoded areas unworked and using colors and stitches indicated, work A, B, D, G, I, J and L, M, O and P pieces according to graphs. Using white for house roof sides and door awning sides, crimson for door sides and tan for interior window sides and Continental Stitch, work C, E, H and N pieces.

2: Omitting attachment edges, with crimson for red edges of house and with matching colors, Overcast edges of A, B, G, L, O and P pieces; with Xmas green, Overcast Santa's glove as indicated on D graph.

3: Using one strand floss, perle coton (work eye stitches four times; see photo) and yarn in colors and embroidery stitches indicated, embroider detail on D, I, O and P pieces as indicated.

4: Whipstitch and assemble pieces and music button according to Santa's Christmas Shoppe Assembly Diagram; hang or display as desired.

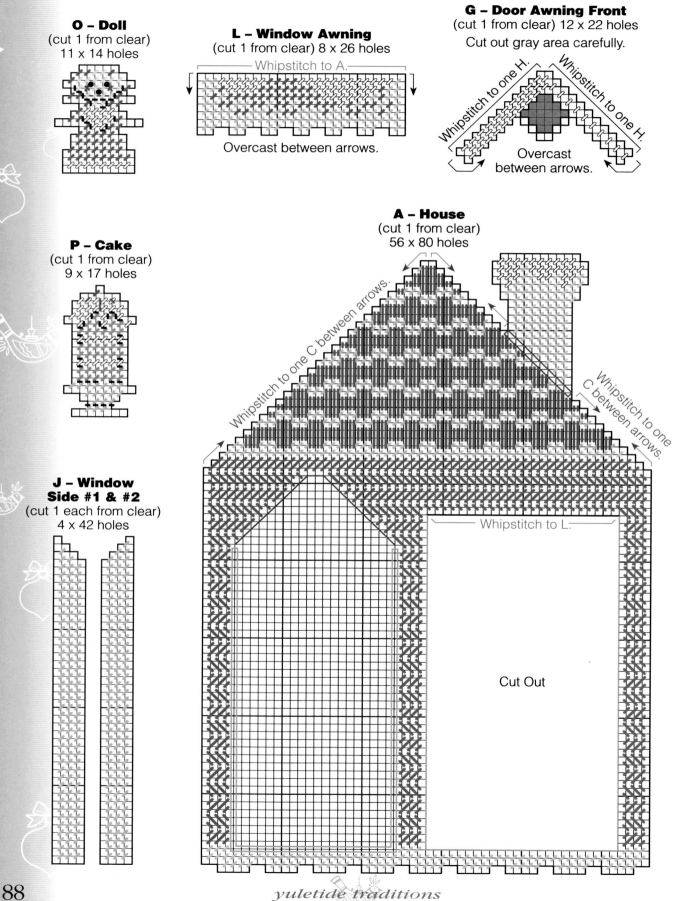

O – Doll
(cut 1 from clear)
11 x 14 holes

L – Window Awning
(cut 1 from clear) 8 x 26 holes
Whipstitch to A.
Overcast between arrows.

G – Door Awning Front
(cut 1 from clear) 12 x 22 holes
Cut out gray area carefully.
Whipstitch to one H.
Whipstitch to one H.
Overcast
between arrows.

A – House
(cut 1 from clear)
56 x 80 holes
Whipstitch to one C between arrows.
Whipstitch to one C between arrows.
Whipstitch to L.
Cut Out

P – Cake
(cut 1 from clear)
9 x 17 holes

**J – Window
Side #1 & #2**
(cut 1 each from clear)
4 x 42 holes

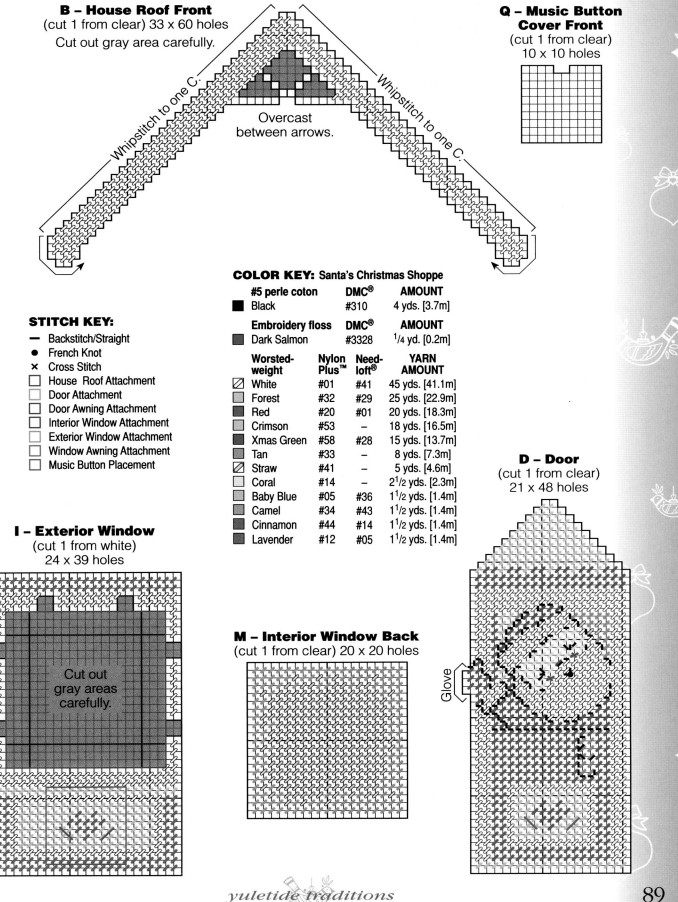

B – House Roof Front
(cut 1 from clear) 33 x 60 holes
Cut out gray area carefully.

Whipstitch to one C.

Whipstitch to one C.

Overcast
between arrows.

**Q – Music Button
Cover Front**
(cut 1 from clear)
10 x 10 holes

STITCH KEY:
— Backstitch/Straight
● French Knot
× Cross Stitch
☐ House Roof Attachment
☐ Door Attachment
☐ Door Awning Attachment
☐ Interior Window Attachment
☐ Exterior Window Attachment
☐ Window Awning Attachment
☐ Music Button Placement

COLOR KEY: Santa's Christmas Shoppe

#5 perle coton		DMC®	AMOUNT
■ Black		#310	4 yds. [3.7m]

Embroidery floss		DMC®	AMOUNT
■ Dark Salmon		#3328	1/4 yd. [0.2m]

Worsted-weight	Nylon Plus™	Need-loft®	YARN AMOUNT
▨ White	#01	#41	45 yds. [41.1m]
☐ Forest	#32	#29	25 yds. [22.9m]
■ Red	#20	#01	20 yds. [18.3m]
☐ Crimson	#53	–	18 yds. [16.5m]
■ Xmas Green	#58	#28	15 yds. [13.7m]
▨ Tan	#33	–	8 yds. [7.3m]
▨ Straw	#41	–	5 yds. [4.6m]
☐ Coral	#14	–	2 1/2 yds. [2.3m]
☐ Baby Blue	#05	#36	1 1/2 yds. [1.4m]
☐ Camel	#34	#43	1 1/2 yds. [1.4m]
■ Cinnamon	#44	#14	1 1/2 yds. [1.4m]
☐ Lavender	#12	#05	1 1/2 yds. [1.4m]

D – Door
(cut 1 from clear)
21 x 48 holes

Glove

I – Exterior Window
(cut 1 from white)
24 x 39 holes

Cut out
gray areas
carefully.

M – Interior Window Back
(cut 1 from clear) 20 x 20 holes

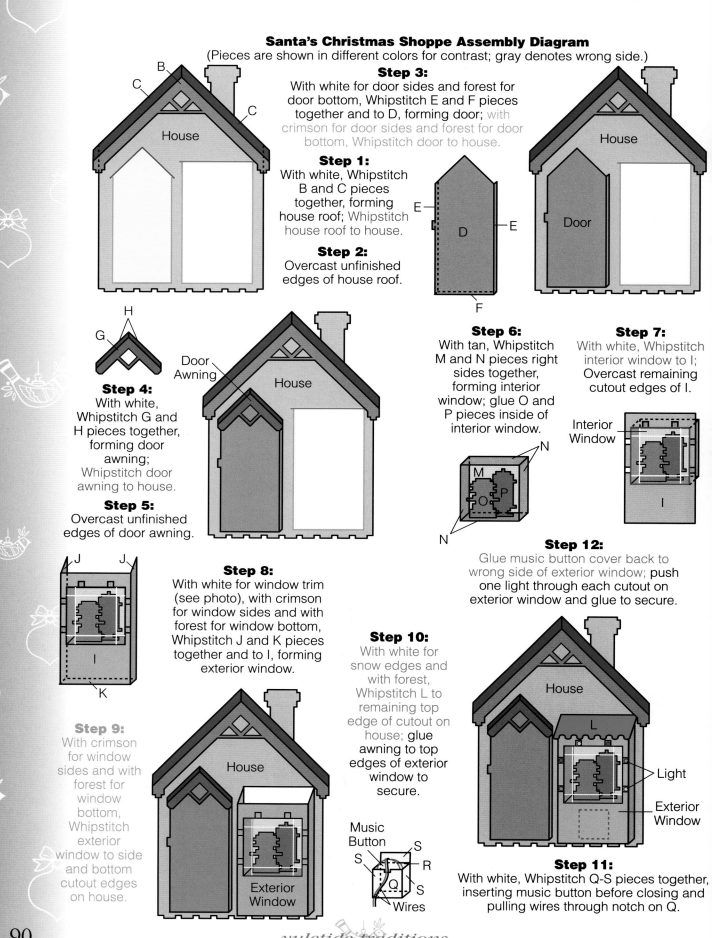

Santa's Christmas Shoppe Assembly Diagram
(Pieces are shown in different colors for contrast; gray denotes wrong side.)

Step 3:
With white for door sides and forest for door bottom, Whipstitch E and F pieces together and to D, forming door; with crimson for door sides and forest for door bottom, Whipstitch door to house.

Step 1:
With white, Whipstitch B and C pieces together, forming house roof; Whipstitch house roof to house.

Step 2:
Overcast unfinished edges of house roof.

Step 4:
With white, Whipstitch G and H pieces together, forming door awning; Whipstitch door awning to house.

Step 5:
Overcast unfinished edges of door awning.

Step 6:
With tan, Whipstitch M and N pieces right sides together, forming interior window; glue O and P pieces inside of interior window.

Step 7:
With white, Whipstitch interior window to I; Overcast remaining cutout edges of I.

Step 8:
With white for window trim (see photo), with crimson for window sides and with forest for window bottom, Whipstitch J and K pieces together and to I, forming exterior window.

Step 9:
With crimson for window sides and with forest for window bottom, Whipstitch exterior window to side and bottom cutout edges on house.

Step 10:
With white for snow edges and with forest, Whipstitch L to remaining top edge of cutout on house; glue awning to top edges of exterior window to secure.

Step 11:
With white, Whipstitch Q-S pieces together, inserting music button before closing and pulling wires through notch on Q.

Step 12:
Glue music button cover back to wrong side of exterior window; push one light through each cutout on exterior window and glue to secure.

silver bells
place mat

designed by
**Mary
Layfield**

silver bells place mat

skill level & size

Average skill level. 12" x 18" tall [30.5cm x 45.7cm].

materials

- Two 12" x 18" [30.5cm x 45.7cm] oval plastic canvas place mats
- 1½ yds. [1.4m] of white/silver 1¼" [32mm] pregathered lace
- Craft glue or glue gun
- Metallic cord; for amount see Color Key.
- Worsted-weight or plastic canvas yarn; for amounts see Color Key.

cutting instructions

For front and backing, use two (one for front and one for backing) place mats.

stitching instructions

NOTE: One place mat is not worked for backing.

1: Using colors and stitches indicated, work one place mat for front according to graph.

2: Using colors and embroidery stitches indicated, embroider detail on front as indicated on graph.

3: Holding backing to wrong side of front, with white, Whipstitch together.

4: Glue lace around outer edges of place mat backing as shown in photo.

COLOR KEY: Silver Bells Place Mat

Metallic cord			AMOUNT
Silver			20 yds. [18.3m]

Worsted-weight	Nylon Plus™	Need-loft®	YARN AMOUNT
White	#01	#41	2½ oz. [70.9g]
Sail Blue	#04	#35	24 yds. [21.9m]
Xmas Green	#58	#28	15 yds. [13.7m]
Xmas Red	#19	#02	12 yds. [11m]
Baby Blue	#05	#36	10 yds. [9.1m]
Forest	#32	#29	8 yds. [7.3m]
Red	#20	#01	6 yds. [5.5m]
Black	#02	#00	2 yds. [1.8m]
Moss	#48	#25	2 yds. [1.8m]

STITCH KEY:
- French Knot

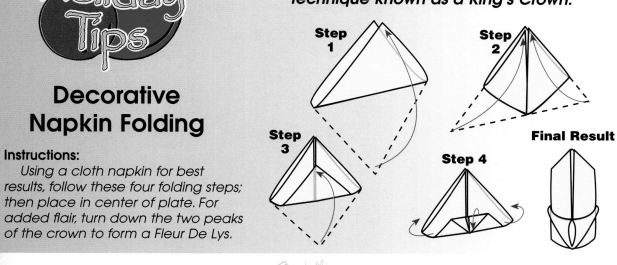

Decorative Napkin Folding

Top off your next holiday table setting with this clever napkin folding technique known as a King's Crown.

Step 1

Step 2

Step 3

Step 4

Final Result

Instructions:

Using a cloth napkin for best results, follow these four folding steps; then place in center of plate. For added flair, turn down the two peaks of the crown to form a Fleur De Lys.

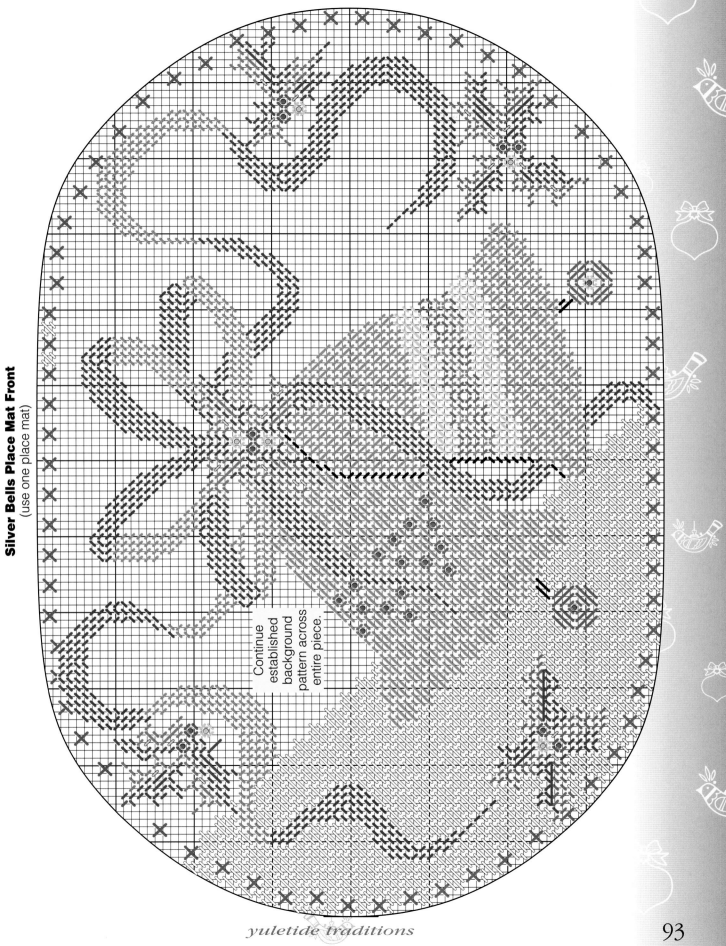

Silver Bells Place Mat Front
(use one place mat)

Continue established background pattern across entire piece.

designed by Mary Layfield

tabletop christmas tree

skill level & size

Challenging skill level. 6¼" x 10½" tall [15.9cm x 26.7cm].

materials

- Two sheets of 7-count plastic canvas
- Two Uniek, Inc. 5" [12.7cm] hexagon shapes
- Assorted beads and charms
- Beading needle and thread
- ½ yd. [0.5m] white 1¼" [32mm] pregathered lace with red rose trim
- Craft glue or glue gun
- Worsted-weight or plastic canvas yarn; for amounts see Color Key.

cutting instructions

A: For tree center branch pieces, cut two according to graph.

B: For tree outer branch pieces, cut eight according to graph.

C: For skirt top and bottom, use two (one for top and one for bottom) hexagon shapes.

D: For blue present sides, cut two 4 x 11 holes.

E: For blue present ends, cut two 4 x 5 holes.

F: For blue present top and bottom, cut two (one for top and one for bottom) 5 x 11 holes.

G: For white present sides, cut four 5 x 5 holes.

H: For white present top and bottom, cut two (one for top and one for bottom) 5 x 5 holes.

I: For green present sides, cut four 5 x 7 holes.

J: For green present top and bottom, cut two (one for top and one for bottom) 7 x 7 holes.

stitching instructions

NOTE: One of each C, F, H and J pieces are not worked for bottoms.

1: Using colors and stitches indicated, work A, B (four on opposite side of canvas), one C for top, D, E, one F for top, G, one H for top, I and

Add a personal touch to your tree by using your old jewelry as the decorations!

Turn your tree into a one-of-a-kind masterpiece full of special memories. Most of us have some old trinkets and beads tucked away in a box that we don't wear anymore, but just can't bear to part with due to that special place they hold in our hearts. Maybe these are things you have collected from your childhood or things that once belonged to a close family member. Perhaps they were a gift from someone that touched your heart in a special way or a brilliant piece of jewelry that has been damaged or broken.

Take those precious treasures out of that old box and personalize your tree with them today! You are sure to have an interesting conversation piece and a chance to share the history and significance of each ornament with others.

one J for top pieces according to graphs.

2: Whipstitch A-C pieces together according to Tree Assembly Diagram; glue lace around outer edges of skirt top as shown in photo.

3: For each present, with matching colors, Whipstitch corresponding pieces together.

NOTE: Cut one 9" [22.9cm] length each of pink and white.

4: Tie each length into a bow; trim ends. Glue pink bow to blue present and white bow to green present. Tie Xmas red yarn around white present and into a bow; trim ends as desired. With beading needle and thread, sew beads and charms to tree and presents to achieve desired effect (see photo). Glue presents to skirt as shown.

I – Green Present Side
(cut 4) 5 x 7 holes

J – Green Present Top & Bottom
(cut 1 each)
7 x 7 holes

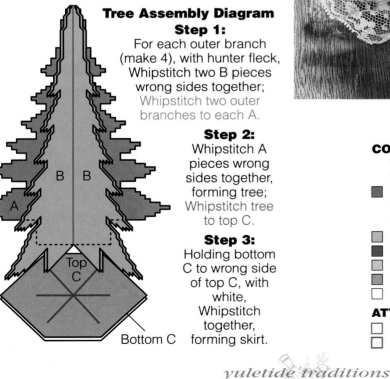

Tree Assembly Diagram
Step 1:
For each outer branch (make 4), with hunter fleck, Whipstitch two B pieces wrong sides together; Whipstitch two outer branches to each A.

Step 2:
Whipstitch A pieces wrong sides together, forming tree; Whipstitch tree to top C.

Step 3:
Holding bottom C to wrong side of top C, with white, Whipstitch together, forming skirt.

Top C

Bottom C

COLOR KEY: Tabletop Christmas Tree

	Worsted-weight	Red Heart®	YARN AMOUNT
■	Hunter Fleck	#4389	3½ oz. [99.2g]

	Worsted-weight	Nylon Plus™	Need-loft®	YARN AMOUNT
■	White	#01	#41	18 yds. [16.5m]
■	Baby Blue	#05	#35	4 yds. [3.7m]
■	Moss	#48	#25	4 yds. [3.7m]
■	Pink	#11	#07	2 yds. [1.8m]
□	Xmas Red	#19	#02	1 yd. [0.9m]

ATTACHMENT KEY:
☐ Tree Outer/Center Branch
☐ Tree/Skirt

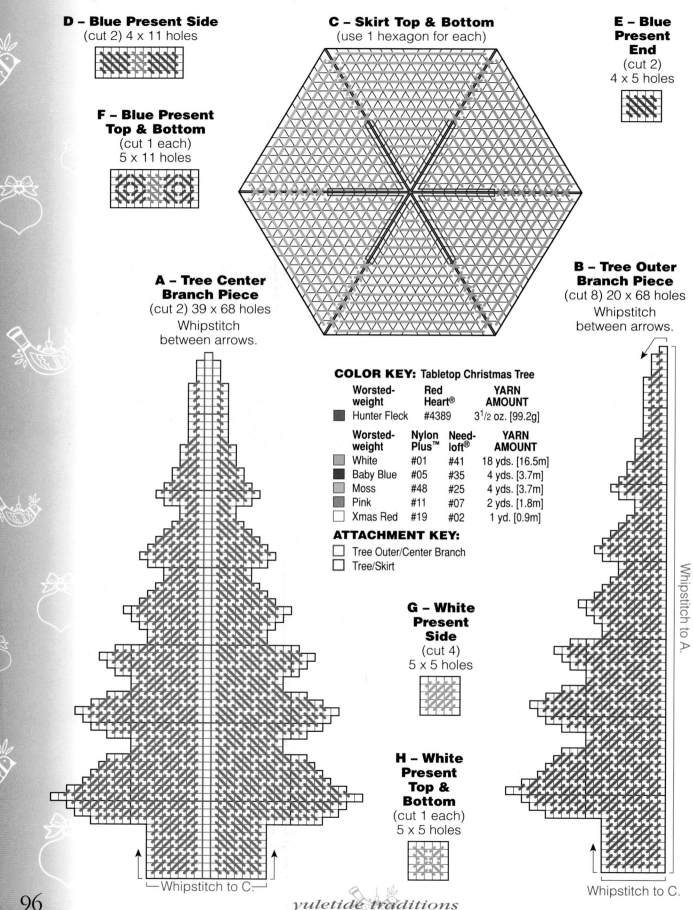

D – Blue Present Side
(cut 2) 4 x 11 holes

C – Skirt Top & Bottom
(use 1 hexagon for each)

E – Blue Present End
(cut 2)
4 x 5 holes

F – Blue Present Top & Bottom
(cut 1 each)
5 x 11 holes

A – Tree Center Branch Piece
(cut 2) 39 x 68 holes
Whipstitch between arrows.

B – Tree Outer Branch Piece
(cut 8) 20 x 68 holes
Whipstitch between arrows.

COLOR KEY: Tabletop Christmas Tree

Worsted-weight	Red Heart®	YARN AMOUNT
■ Hunter Fleck	#4389	3 1/2 oz. [99.2g]

Worsted-weight	Nylon Plus™	Need-loft®	YARN AMOUNT
White	#01	#41	18 yds. [16.5m]
Baby Blue	#05	#35	4 yds. [3.7m]
Moss	#48	#25	4 yds. [3.7m]
Pink	#11	#07	2 yds. [1.8m]
Xmas Red	#19	#02	1 yd. [0.9m]

ATTACHMENT KEY:
☐ Tree Outer/Center Branch
☐ Tree/Skirt

G – White Present Side
(cut 4)
5 x 5 holes

H – White Present Top & Bottom
(cut 1 each)
5 x 5 holes

Whipstitch to A.

└─ Whipstitch to C.

Whipstitch to C.

advent
calendar

designed by
**Mike
Vickery**

skill level & size
Average skill level. 12" x 18" [30.5cm x 45.7cm].

materials
- One 12" x 18" [30.5cm x 45.7cm] or larger sheet of 7-count plastic canvas
- 6 yds. [5.5m] white ¹⁄₁₆" [2mm] satin ribbon
- 24 individually-wrapped candies
- Metallic cord; for amount see Color Key.
- Worsted-weight or plastic canvas yarn; for amounts see Color Key.

cutting instructions
For Advent Calender, use one 80 x 120-hole sheet.

stitching instructions
1: Using colors and stitches indicated, work Advent Calender according to graph; fill in uncoded areas using white and Continental Stitch. With metallic cord, Overcast edges.
NOTE: Cut ribbon into twenty-four 9" [22.9cm] lengths.
2: For each candy bow, thread one ribbon

Advent Calendar (use 80 x 120 hole sheet)

Pattern is divided onto two pages.

through canvas at center top of each number (see photo); pull ends to even and tie into an overhand knot close to canvas. Tie ends into a bow over one end of candy wrapper to hold in place. ✻

COLOR KEY: Advent Calendar

	Metallic cord			AMOUNT
■	Gold			15 yds. [13.7m]

	Worsted-weight	Nylon Plus™	Need-loft®	YARN AMOUNT
□	White	#01	#41	45 yds. [41.1m]
■	Xmas Red	#19	#02	30 yds. [27.4m]
▨	Holly	#31	#27	20 yds. [18.3m]
▨	Sandstone	#47	#16	18 yds. [16.5m]
■	Bright Purple	–	#64	15 yds. [13.7m]
▨	Yellow	#26	#57	13 yds. [11.9m]
▨	Fern	#57	#23	10 yds. [9.1m]

	Worsted-weight	Nylon Plus™	Need-loft®	YARN AMOUNT
■	Forest	#32	#29	10 yds. [9.1m]
▨	Bright Blue	–	#60	8 yds. [7.3m]
▨	Gray	#23	#38	8 yds. [7.3m]
■	Camel	#34	#43	7 yds. [6.4m]
□	Red	#20	#01	5 yds. [4.6m]
□	Crimson	#53	–	4 yds. [3.7m]
□	Gold	#27	#17	4 yds. [3.7m]

	Worsted-weight	Nylon Plus™	Need-loft®	YARN AMOUNT
■	Brown	#36	#15	3 yds. [2.7m]
▨	Purple	#21	#46	3 yds. [2.7m]
▨	Silver	–	#37	3 yds. [2.7m]
▨	Tangerine	#15	#11	3 yds. [2.7m]
■	Black	#02	#00	2 yds. [1.8m]
▨	Pumpkin	#50	#12	2 yds. [1.8m]
■	Royal	#09	#32	2 yds. [1.8m]

Open-edge row repeated on both pages.

Share the glow of Christmas love as our happy snow couple guides us through a glimmering trail of plastic canvas family favorites. Be on the lookout for projects like the Candy Cane Holder and the Decorative Holly set that are sure to tickle the tummies of the whole family.

designed by
Christine A. Hendricks

mistletoe & magic

skill level & size

Average skill level. 13½" x 18" [34.3cm x 45.7cm].

materials

- One 13½" x 22½" [34.3cm x 57.2cm] sheet of 7-count plastic canvas
- Six-strand embroidery floss; for amount see Color Key.
- Worsted-weight or plastic canvas yarn; for amounts see Color Key.

cutting instructions

For Mistletoe and Magic, cut one 88 x 118 holes.

stitching instructions

1: Using colors and stitches indicated, work according to graph; fill in uncoded areas using white and Continental Stitch. With white, Overcast edges.

2: Using three strands black floss and embroidery stitches indicated, embroider detail as indicated on graph.

3: Hang or display as desired.

COLOR KEY: Mistletoe & Magic

Embroidery floss		DMC®	AMOUNT
■ Black		#310	16 yds. [14.6m]

Worsted-weight	Nylon Plus™	Need-loft®	YARN AMOUNT
White	#01	#41	2½ oz. [70.9g]
Flesh Tone	–	#56	15 yds. [13.7m]
Baby Green	#28	–	12 yds. [11m]
Holly	#31	#27	10 yds. [9.1m]
Sail Blue	#04	#35	8 yds. [7.3m]
Camel	#34	#43	6 yds. [5.5m]
Silver	–	#37	6 yds. [5.5m]
Denim	#06	–	5 yds. [4.6m]
Lemon	#25	#20	4 yds. [3.7m]
Pumpkin	#50	#12	4 yds. [3.7m]
Yellow	#26	#57	4 yds. [3.7m]
Black	#02	#00	3 yds. [2.7m]
Bright Purple	–	#64	3 yds. [2.7m]
Lilac	#22	#45	3 yds. [2.7m]
Lavender	#12	#05	1 yd. [0.9m]
Pink	#11	#07	1 yd. [0.9m]
Royal Dark	#07	#48	1 yd. [0.9m]
Tangerine	#15	#11	1 yd. [0.9m]

STITCH KEY:
- — Backstitch/Straight
- × Cross
- ● French Knot

102

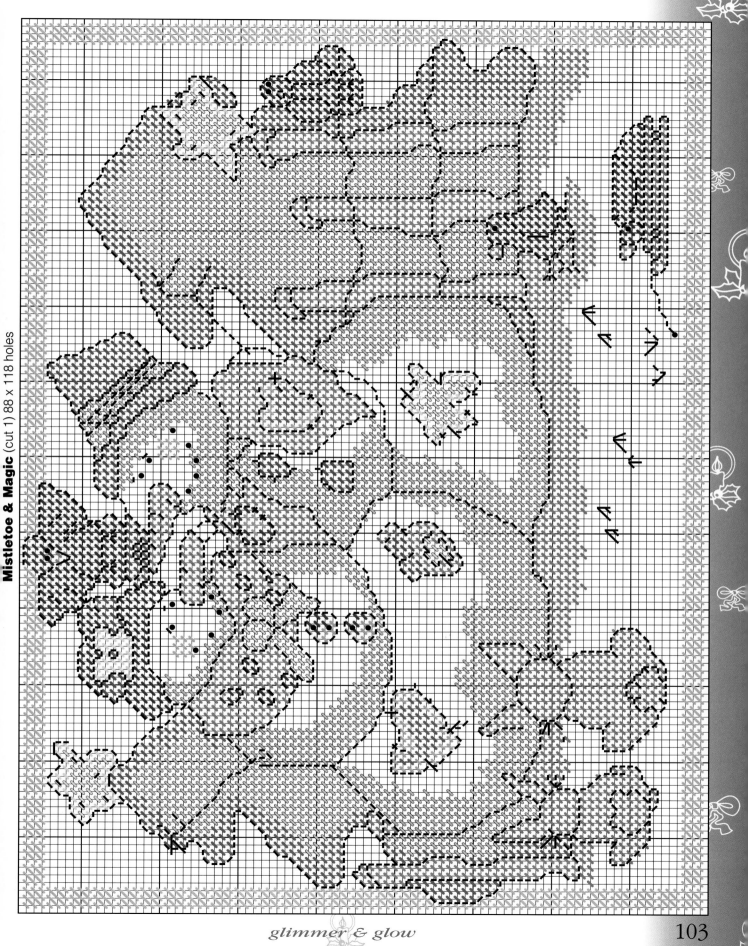

holly holiday *runner*

designed by
Kristine Loffredo

skill level & size

Average skill level. 7" x 26" [17.8cm x 66cm].

materials

- Two sheets of 7-count plastic canvas
- 36 red 6mm faceted beads
- Craft glue or glue gun
- Metallic cord; for amount see Color Key
- Worsted-weight or plastic canvas yarn; for amounts see Color Key.

cutting instructions

For Holly Runner Pieces, cut one each according to graphs.

stitching instructions

1: Overlapping ends as indicated on graphs and working through both thicknesses at overlap area to join, using colors and stitches indicated, work pieces according to graphs.

2: With Xmas green for leaves and white for remaining edges, Overcast edges of Holly Runner.

3: Glue beads to Holly Runner as indicated on graph.

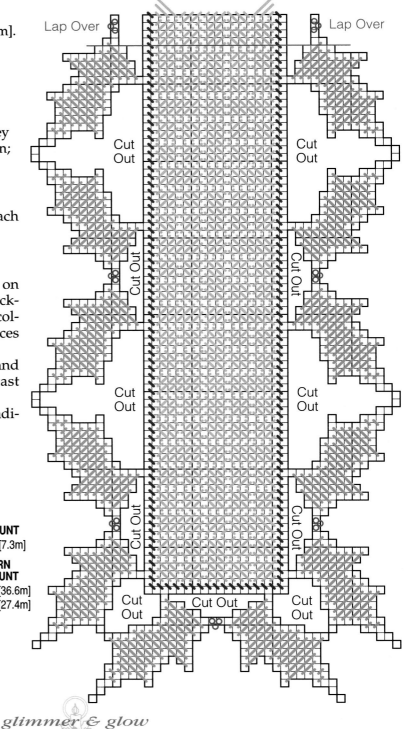

Holly Runner Piece #1
(cut 1) 46 x 89 holes

Lap Over   Lap Over

Cut Out   Cut Out

Cut Out   Cut Out

Cut Out   Cut Out

Cut Out   Cut Out

Cut Out   Cut Out   Cut Out

COLOR KEY: Holly Holiday Runner

Metallic cord			AMOUNT
■ Red/Black			8 yds. [7.3m]

Worsted-weight	Nylon Plus™	Need-loft®	YARN AMOUNT
■ Christmas Green	#58	#28	40 yds. [36.6m]
▨ White	#01	#41	30 yds. [27.4m]

ATTACHMENT:
○ Bead

Coordinating picture frame on page 107.

glimmer & glow

Holly Runner Piece #2
(cut 1) 46 x 89 holes

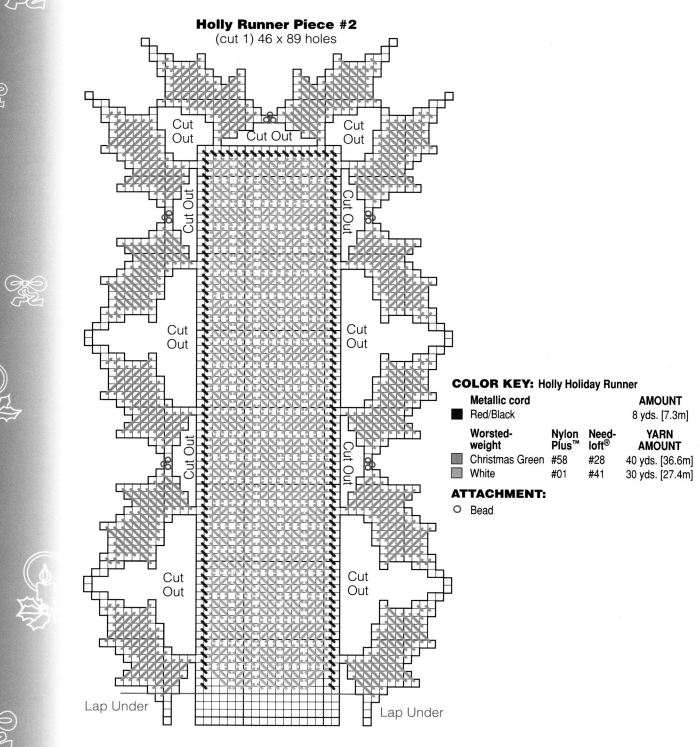

COLOR KEY: Holly Holiday Runner

Metallic cord			AMOUNT
■ Red/Black			8 yds. [7.3m]

Worsted-weight	Nylon Plus™	Need-loft®	YARN AMOUNT
Christmas Green	#58	#28	40 yds. [36.6m]
White	#01	#41	30 yds. [27.4m]

ATTACHMENT:
○ Bead

holly holiday *frame*

designed by Kristine Loffredo

skill level & size

Average skill level. 5" x 13" [12.7cm x 33cm].

materials

- 1½ sheets of 7-count plastic canvas
- Nine red 6mm faceted beads
- Craft glue or glue gun
- Metallic cord; for amounts see Color Key on page 108.
- Worsted-weight or plastic canvas yarn; for amounts see Color Key.

cutting instructions

A: For Frame front, cut one according to graph.

B: For leaves, cut three according to graph.

C: For Frame backings, cut three according to graph.

stitching instructions

NOTE: C pieces are not worked.

1: Using colors and stitches indicated, work A and B pieces according to graphs; with metallic green/gold for cutouts and with Xmas green, Overcast tree cutout edges of A and outer edges of B pieces.

2: Whipstitch A and C pieces together as indicated and according to Frame Assembly Ilustration; Overcast remaining unfinished edges of A.

3: Glue three beads to each B as indicated on graph; glue leaves to frame front as indicated and as shown in photo.

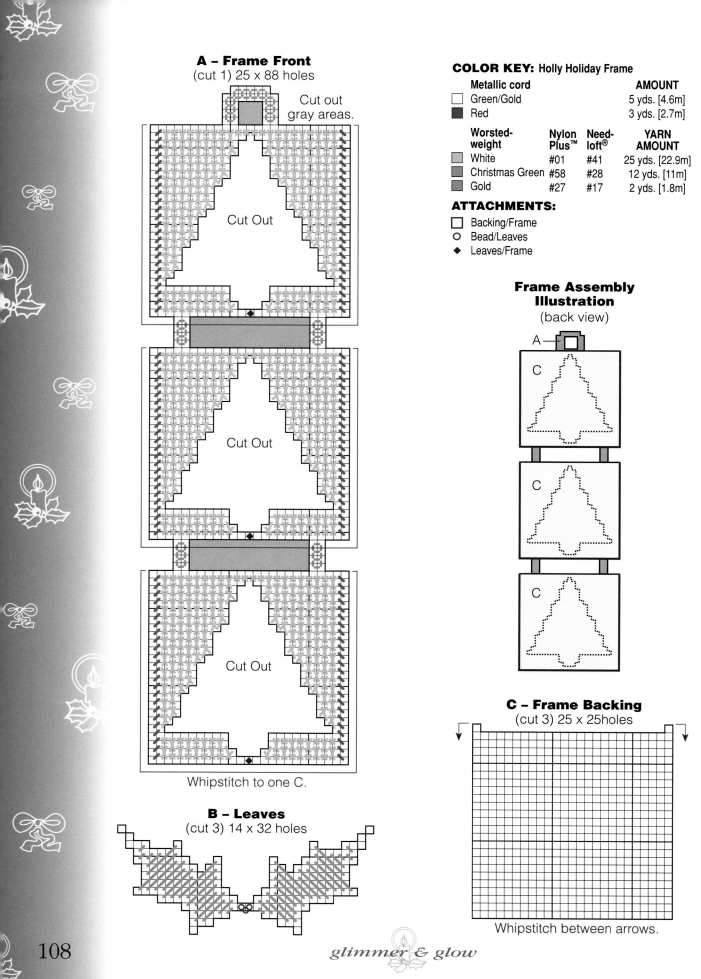

A – Frame Front
(cut 1) 25 x 88 holes

Cut out gray areas.

Cut Out

Cut Out

Cut Out

Whipstitch to one C.

B – Leaves
(cut 3) 14 x 32 holes

COLOR KEY: Holly Holiday Frame

Metallic cord			AMOUNT
Green/Gold			5 yds. [4.6m]
Red			3 yds. [2.7m]

Worsted-weight	Nylon Plus™	Need-loft®	YARN AMOUNT
White	#01	#41	25 yds. [22.9m]
Christmas Green	#58	#28	12 yds. [11m]
Gold	#27	#17	2 yds. [1.8m]

ATTACHMENTS:

☐ Backing/Frame
○ Bead/Leaves
◆ Leaves/Frame

Frame Assembly Illustration
(back view)

A

C

C

C

C – Frame Backing
(cut 3) 25 x 25 holes

Whipstitch between arrows.

argyle mug insert & coaster

designed by
Angie Arickx

skill level & size

Average skill level. Mug Insert fits inside a 4" tall [10.2cm] plastic snap-together mug; Coaster is 3¼" [8.2cm] square.

materials

- ½ sheet of 7-count plastic canvas
- Snap-together mug
- ⅛" [3mm] metallic ribbon or metallic cord; for amount see Color Key.
- Worsted-weight or plastic canvas yarn; for amounts see Color Key.

cutting instructions

A: For Mug Insert, cut one 23 x 64 holes.
B: For Coaster, cut one 21 x 21 holes.

stitching instructions

1: Using colors and stitches indicated, work pieces according to graphs. With white, Overcast edges of B.

2: With white, Whipstitch short ends of Mug Insert together as indicated on graph; Overcast unfinished edges. Place Insert inside mug according to manufacturer's instructions.

COLOR KEY: Argyle Mug Insert & Coaster

⅛" ribbon or cord		Rainbow Gallery	AMOUNT
Gold		#PC1	8 yds. [7.3m]

Worsted-weight	Nylon Plus™	Need-loft®	YARN AMOUNT
White	#01	#41	12 yds. [11m]
Gold	#27	#17	10 yds. [9.1m]
Holly	#31	#27	8 yds. [7.3m]
Red	#20	#01	8 yds. [7.3m]

B – Coaster
(cut 1) 21 x 21 holes

A – Mug Insert
(cut 1) 23 x 64 holes

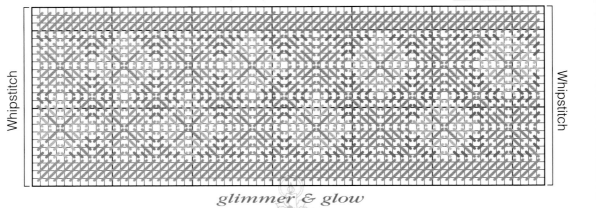

Whipstitch

Whipstitch

glimmer & glow

109

designed by
**Michele
Wilcox**

santa's *candy cane* holder

skill level & size

Average skill level. 4½" x 4½" x 5½" tall [11.4cm x 11.4cm x 14cm], not including embellishments.

materials

- 1½ sheets of 7-count plastic canvas
- 21 red 5mm sew-on sequins
- 21 clear seed beads
- 9mm gold jingle bell
- Sewing needle and red thread
- Craft glue or glue gun
- #3 perle coton or six-strand embroidery floss; for amount see Color Key.
- Worsted-weight or plastic canvas yarn; for amounts see Color Key.

cutting instructions

A: For sides, cut four 30 x 36 holes.
B: For bottom, cut one 30 x 30 holes (no graph).
C: For wreath, cut one according to graph.
D: For mouse head, cut one according to graph.
E: For mouse ears, cut two according to graph.
F: For mouse paws, cut two according to graph.
G: For mouse feet, cut two according to graph.
H: For mouse tail, cut one according to graph.

stitching instructions

NOTE: B piece is not worked.
1: Using colors and stitches indicated, work A and C-H pieces according to graphs; with matching colors, Overcast edges of C-H pieces.
2: Using perle coton or six strands floss and French knot, embroider eyes and nose on D as indicated on graph.
3: With white, Whipstitch A and B pieces together, forming Holder; Overcast unfinished edges.
4: With thread, sew seed beads and sequins to C as indicated and according to Sequin Attachment Illustration.

NOTE: Cut a 6" length of red yarn.
5: Tie yarn into a bow around H piece as shown in photo; glue bell to ◆ hole on mouse tail as indicated.
6: Glue C-H pieces to one side of Holder as shown.

Sequin Attachment Illustration

Bead
Sequin

D – Mouse Head
(cut 1)
7 x 9 holes

E – Mouse Ear
(cut 2)
7 x 7 holes

A – Side
(cut 4) 30 x 36 holes

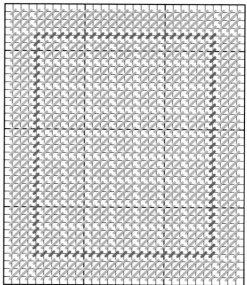

COLOR KEY: Santa's Candy Cane Holder

#3 perle coton or floss		DMC®	AMOUNT
■ Black		#310	1 yd. [0.9m]

Worsted-weight	Nylon Plus™	Need-loft®	YARN AMOUNT
☐ White	#01	#41	80 yds. [73.2m]
▨ Red	#20	#01	10 yds. [9.1m]
▨ Christmas Green	#58	#28	10 yds. [9.1m]
▨ Pewter	#40	–	6 yds. [5.5m]
☐ Coral	#14	–	1 yd. [0.9m]

STITCH KEY:

● French Knot
○ Sequin Attachment
◆ Bell Placement

F – Mouse Paw
(cut 2)
4 x 4 holes

G – Mouse Foot
(cut 2)
5 x 5 holes

H – Mouse Tail
(cut 1)
3 x 15 holes

C – Wreath
(cut 1) 26 x 28 holes

Cut Out

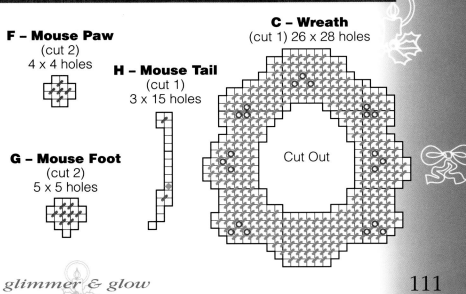

designed by
Nancy Dorman

panda tissue cover

skill level & size

Average skill level. Snugly covers a boutique-style tissue box.

materials

- Two sheets of 10-count plastic canvas
- ¼ yd. [0.2m] of red ⅛" [3mm] satin ribbon
- Craft glue or glue gun
- Medium metallic braid or metallic cord; for amount see Color Key.
- 2-ply or sport-weight yarn; for amounts see Color Key.

cutting instructions

A: For sides, cut four 45 x 57 holes.
B: For top, cut one according to graph.
C: For panda, cut one according to graph.

B – Top
(cut 1) 45 x 45 holes

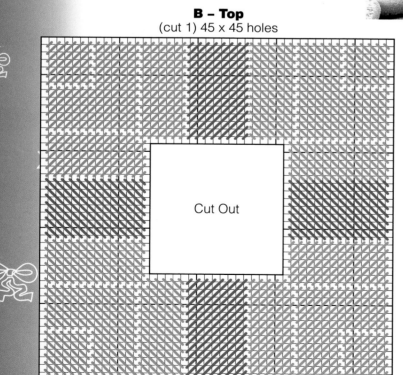

Cut Out

stitching instructions

1: Using colors and stitches indicated, work pieces according to graphs; fill in un-coded areas of C using white and Continental Stitch. With matching colors as shown in photo, Overcast edges of C and cutout edges of B.

2: Using braid or cord and yarn in colors and stitches indicated, embroider detail on C as indicated on graph.

3: With matching colors and Herringbone Whipstitch, Whipstitch A and B pieces together, forming Cover. With Herringbone Overcast, Overcast unfinished edges.

NOTE: Cut two 9" [22.9cm] lengths of gold and one 9" length of red yarn.

4: Tie each strand into a bow. Glue bows to C as indicated; matching bottom edges, glue panda to one Cover side.

A – Side (cut 4) 45 x 57 holes

COLOR KEY: Panda Bear Tissue Cover

Med. metallic braid or cord	AMOUNT
Gold	1 yd. [0.9m]

Sport-weight	YARN AMOUNT
Holly	3 oz. [85.1g]
Red	28 yds. [25.6m]
Black	20 yds. [18.3m]
White	12 yds. [11m]

STITCH KEY:

— Backstitch/Straight

ATTACHMENTS:

◆ Metallic Bow
◆ Yarn Bow
◆ Satin Bow

C – Panda
(cut 1) 73 x 83 holes

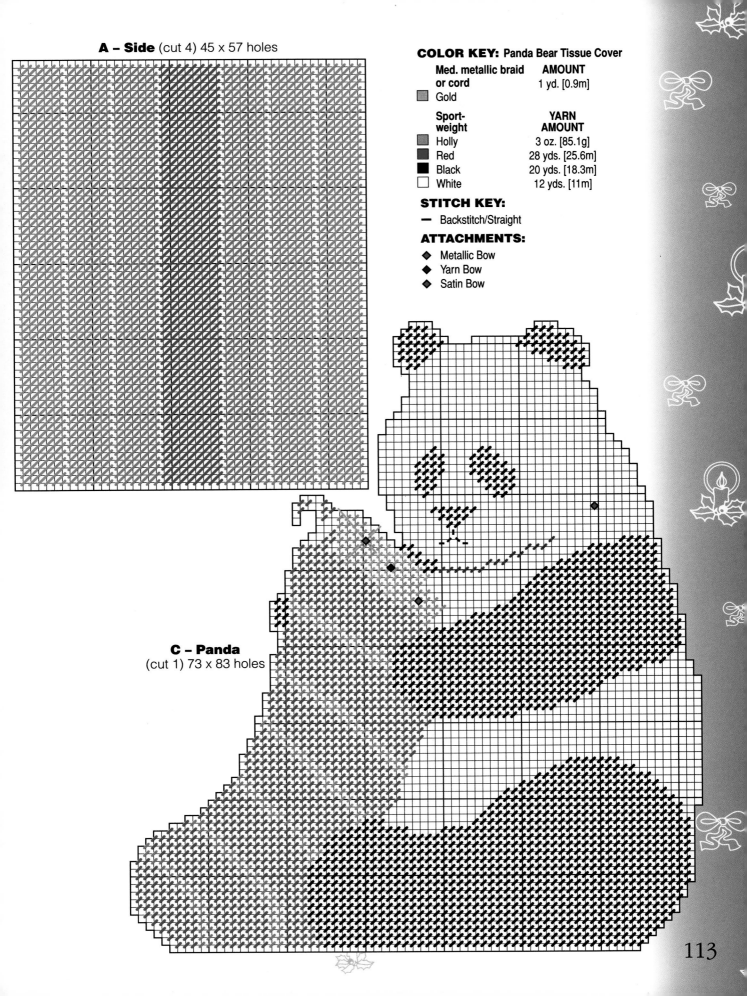

designed by
Sheri
Lautenschlager

jolly candles

skill level & sizes

Challenging skill level. Ornament is 3½" x 4½" [8.9cm x 11.4cm]; Match Holder is 2¾" x 5" x 10" tall [7cm x 12.7cm x 25.4cm]; Wreath is 12" [30.5cm] across.

materials

- Five sheets of 7-count plastic canvas
- 21 red 15mm round stones
- Four red 7mm round stones
- Seven red 5mm round stones
- One 18mm x 13mm topaz pear stone
- Two 14mm x 10mm topaz pear stones
- Four oval 12mm wiggle eyes
- Two oval 18mm wiggle eyes
- Craft glue or glue gun
- Six-strand embroidery floss; for amounts see Color Key.
- Worsted-weight or plastic canvas yarn; for amounts see Color Key.

cutting instructions

A: For Ornament pieces, cut two according to graph.

B: For Ornament leaf pieces, cut two according to graph.

C: For small bow tie pieces, cut four according to graph.

D: For Match Holder candle pieces, cut two according to graph.

E: For Match Holder side pieces, cut eight 13 x 49 holes.

F: For Match Holder bottom pieces, cut two 13 x 13 holes.

G: For Match Holder leaf pieces, cut two according to graph.

H: For large bow tie pieces, cut two according to graph.

I: For Wreath pieces, cut two, according to graph.

J: For Wreath leaf pieces, cut twelve according to graph.

cutting instructions

1: Using colors and stitches indicated, work A, B and D-I (hold corresponding pieces together and work through both thicknesses as one) pieces according to graphs. For each small bow tie (make 2), hold two C pieces together and work through both thicknesses as one; for each wreath leaves (make 6), repeat as above with two J pieces. With matching colors, Whipstitch unfinished edges of A-D and G-J pieces.

2: Using three strands floss and yarn (Separate into individual plies, if desired.) in colors and embroidery stitches indicated, embroider detail on A, B, D and G-J pieces as indicated on graphs.

3: For Match Box, with red, Whipstitch E and F pieces together; Whipstitch unfinished edges together. Matching bottom edges, glue D to one side as shown in photo. Glue wreath leaves around I as shown.

4: Glue remaining pieces, wiggle eyes and round stones together as indicated and as shown. Glue large pear stone to Match Holder Candle and one small pear stone to each remaining candle as shown. ⚜

COLOR KEY: Jolly Candles

Embroidery floss			AMOUNT
■ Black			2 yds. [1.8m]
■ Ecru			1 yd. [0.9m]

Worsted-weight	Nylon Plus™	Need-loft®	YARN AMOUNT
Christmas Red	#19	#02	35 yds. [32m]
Holly	#31	#27	30 yds. [27.4m]
Christmas Green	#58	#28	10 yds. [9.1m]
Burgundy	#13	#03	3 yds. [2.7m]
Tangerine	#15	#11	3 yds. [2.7m]
Bright Pink	–	#62	½ yd. [0.5m]

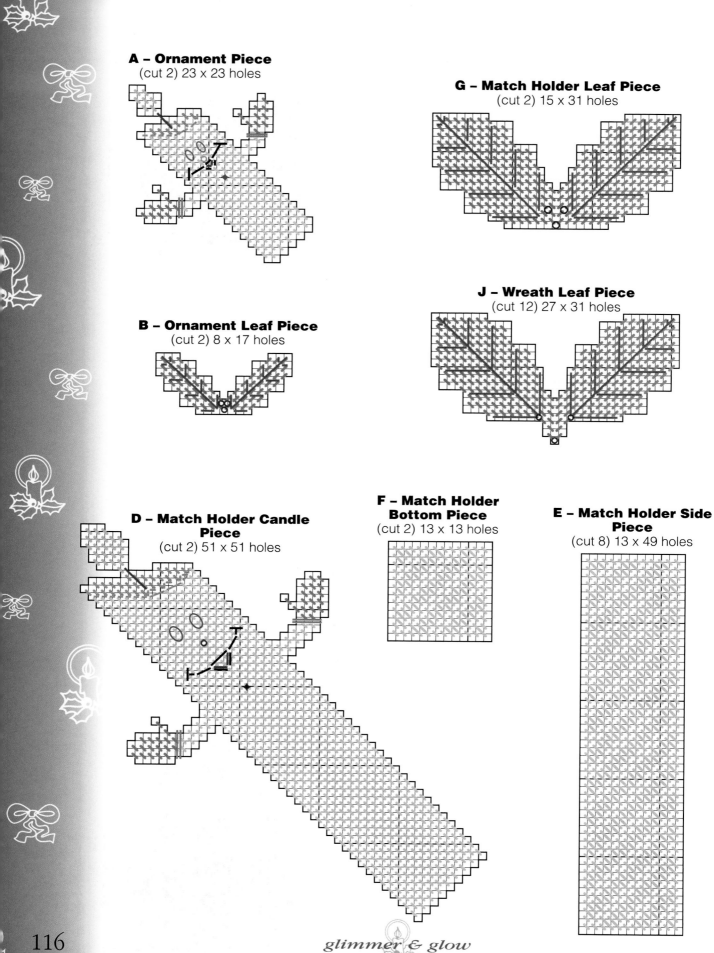

A – Ornament Piece
(cut 2) 23 x 23 holes

B – Ornament Leaf Piece
(cut 2) 8 x 17 holes

D – Match Holder Candle Piece
(cut 2) 51 x 51 holes

G – Match Holder Leaf Piece
(cut 2) 15 x 31 holes

J – Wreath Leaf Piece
(cut 12) 27 x 31 holes

F – Match Holder Bottom Piece
(cut 2) 13 x 13 holes

E – Match Holder Side Piece
(cut 8) 13 x 49 holes

glimmer & glow

COLOR KEY: Jolly Candles

Embroidery floss			AMOUNT
■ Black			2 yds. [1.8m]
■ Ecru			1 yd. [0.9m]

Worsted-weight	Nylon Plus™	Need-loft®	YARN AMOUNT
☐ Christmas Red	#19	#02	35 yds. [32m]
☐ Holly	#31	#27	30 yds. [27.4m]
☐ Christmas Green	#58	#28	10 yds. [9.1m]
☐ Burgundy	#13	#03	3 yds. [2.7m]
☐ Tangerine	#15	#11	3 yds. [2.7m]
☐ Bright Pink	–	#62	1/2 yd. [0.5m]

STITCH KEY:
- — Backstitch/Straight
- ○ 5mm Stones
- ○ 7mm Stones
- ○ 15mm Stones
- ○ 18mm Wiggle Eyes
- ○ 12mm Wiggle Eyes

PLACEMENTS:
- ✦ Large Bow
- ✦ Small Bow

C – Small Bow Tie Piece
(cut 4) 4 x 4 holes

I – Wreath Piece
(cut 2)
60 x 60 holes

Cut Out

H – Large Bow Tie Piece
(cut 2) 8 x 8 holes

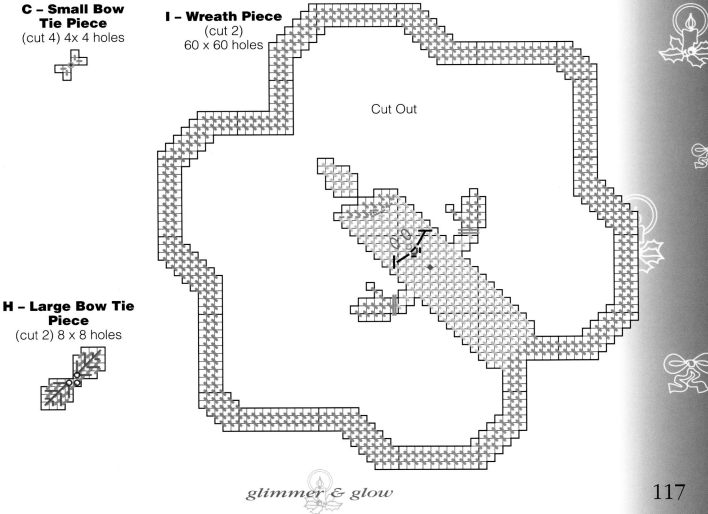

designed by
Kimberly A. Suber

santa's *meowy* christmas

skill level & size

Average skill level. 10¼" x 13" [26cm x 33cm].

materials

- 2½ sheets of 7-count plastic canvas
- Eight gold ¼" [6mm] jingle bells
- Craft glue or glue gun
- Worsted-weight or plastic canvas yarn; for amounts see Color Key.

cutting instructions

A: For base, cut one 67 x 85 holes.

B: For cat #1 and #2, cut one each according to graphs.

C: For poinsettias, cut six according to graph.

D: For leaves, cut six according to graph.

E: For cat collars, cut two 1 x 9 holes.

F: For letters, cut number needed to spell "Meowy Christmas" according to graphs.

stitching instructions

1: Using colors and stitches indicated, work A-E (substitute red for holly on one E) pieces according to graphs; fill in uncoded areas of B#2 using gray and Continental Stitch. With matching colors, Overcast edges of A-E pieces.

2: Alternating red and holly as desired or as shown in photo, Overcast edges of F pieces. Using white and stitches indicated, work F pieces according to graphs.

3: Using colors (Separate yarn into individual plies, if desired.) and embroidery stitches indicated, embroider detail on A, B and three C pieces.

4: Glue four bells to each collar as indicated; glue one collar to each cat and cats to base (see photo).

5: For each poinsettia (make 3), glue two of each C together (see photo). Glue poinsettias, leaves and letters to base as shown.

6: Hang as desired.

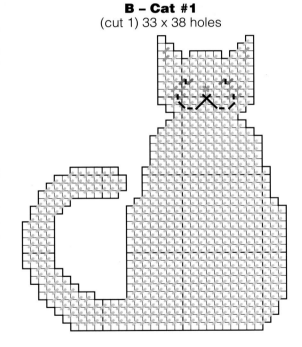

B – Cat #1
(cut 1) 33 x 38 holes

COLOR KEY: Santa's Meowy Christmas

Worsted-weight	Nylon Plus™	Need-loft®	YARN AMOUNT
Baby Blue	#05	#36	60 yds. [54.9m]
Royal	#09	#32	50 yds. [45.7m]
White	#01	#41	20 yds. [18.3m]
Gray	#23	#38	20 yds. [18.3m]
Red	#20	#01	20 yds. [18.3m]
Tangerine	#15	#11	15 yds. [13.7m]
Holly	#31	#27	10 yds. [9.1m]
Black	#02	#00	1 yd. [0.9m]
Bright Blue	–	#60	1 yd. [0.9m]
Lavender	#12	#05	1 yd. [0.9m]
Lime	#29	–	1 yd. [0.9m]

STITCH KEY:

- — Backstitch/Straight
- ● French Knot
- ◆ Bell Attachment

D – Leaf
(cut 6) 7 x 12 holes

E – Cat Collar
(cut 2) 1 x 9 holes

C – Poinsettia
(cut 6) 17 x 17 holes

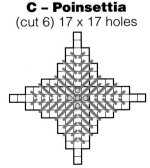

COLOR KEY: Santa's Meowy Christmas

Worsted-weight	Nylon Plus™	Need-loft®	YARN AMOUNT
Baby Blue	#05	#36	60 yds. [54.9m]
Royal	#09	#32	50 yds. [45.7m]
White	#01	#41	20 yds. [18.3m]
Gray	#23	#38	20 yds. [18.3m]
Red	#20	#01	20 yds. [18.3m]
Tangerine	#15	#11	15 yds. [13.7m]
Holly	#31	#27	10 yds. [9.1m]
Black	#02	#00	1 yd. [0.9m]
Bright Blue	–	#60	1 yd. [0.9m]
Lavender	#12	#05	1 yd. [0.9m]
Lime	#29	–	1 yd. [0.9m]

STITCH KEY:

— Backstitch/Straight

● French Knot

◆ Bell Attachment

B – Cat #2
(cut 1) 33 x 38 holes

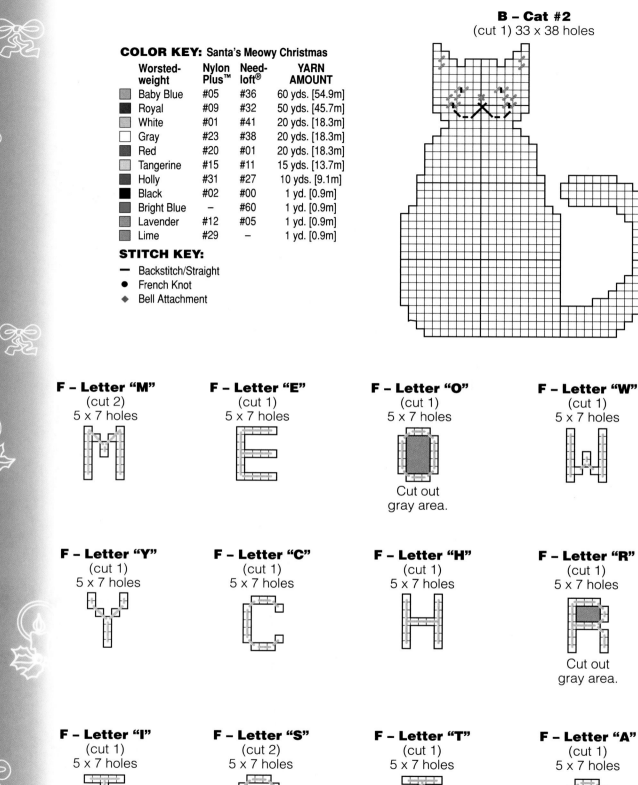

F – Letter "M"
(cut 2)
5 x 7 holes

F – Letter "E"
(cut 1)
5 x 7 holes

F – Letter "O"
(cut 1)
5 x 7 holes

Cut out
gray area.

F – Letter "W"
(cut 1)
5 x 7 holes

F – Letter "Y"
(cut 1)
5 x 7 holes

F – Letter "C"
(cut 1)
5 x 7 holes

F – Letter "H"
(cut 1)
5 x 7 holes

F – Letter "R"
(cut 1)
5 x 7 holes

Cut out
gray area.

F – Letter "I"
(cut 1)
5 x 7 holes

F – Letter "S"
(cut 2)
5 x 7 holes

F – Letter "T"
(cut 1)
5 x 7 holes

F – Letter "A"
(cut 1)
5 x 7 holes

Cut out
gray area.

A – Base (cut 1) 67 x 85 holes

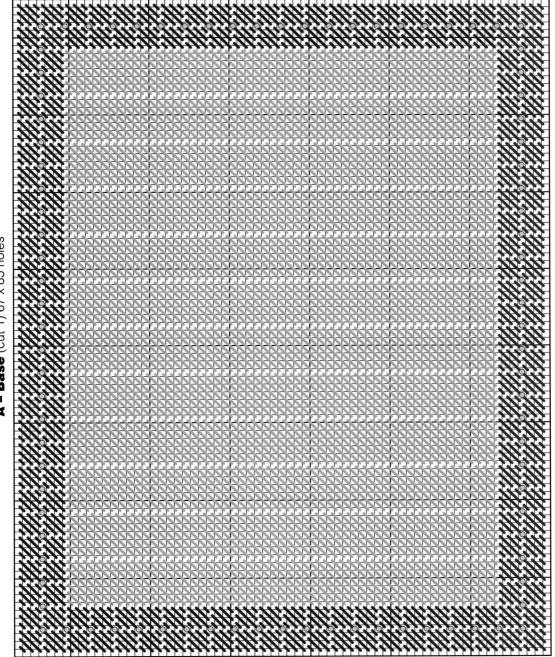

The plastic canvas angels have gathered a heavenly selection of stitching delights for us to enjoy on our magical path. It seems as though they glisten with a touch of angel dust, or could those be freshly fallen snowflakes?

angel
gathering

designed by
Christine A. Hendricks

snow angels

skill level & size

Average skill level. 12¼" x 17¾" [31.1cm x 45.1cm].

materials

- One 13½" x 22½" [34.3cm x 57.2cm] sheet of 7-count plastic canvas
- #12 tapestry braid or metallic cord; for amount see Color Key.
- Six-strand embroidery floss; for amount see Color Key.
- Worsted-weight or plastic canvas yarn; for amounts see Color Key.

cutting instructions

For Snow Angels, cut one 81 x 118 holes.

stitching instructions

1: Using colors and stitches indicated, work according to graph; fill in uncoded areas using white and Continental Stitch. With dark royal,

COLOR KEY: Snow Angels

Metallic braid or cord	Kreinik Tapestry™		AMOUNT
Gold	#002		½ yd. [0.5m]
Embroidery floss	**DMC®**		**AMOUNT**
Black	#310		25 yds. [22.9m]

Worsted-weight	Nylon Plus™	Need-loft®	YARN AMOUNT
White	#01	#41	2½ oz. [70.6g]
Dark Royal	#07	#48	23 yds. [21m]
Christmas Green	#58	#28	23 yds. [21m]
Red	#20	#01	14 yds. [12.8m]
Flesh Tone	–	#56	10 yds. [9.1m]
Sail Blue	#04	#35	10 yds. [9.1m]
Baby Green	#28	–	9 yds. [8.2m]
Lemon	#25	#20	3 yds. [2.7m]
Bright Purple	–	#64	2 yds. [1.8m]
Lilac	#22	#45	2 yds. [1.8m]
Maple	#35	#13	2 yds. [1.8m]
Gray	#23	#38	1 yd. [0.9m]
Pumpkin	#50	#12	1 yd. [0.9m]
Yellow	#26	#57	1 yd. [0.9m]
Orchid	#56	#44	½ yd. [0.5m]

STITCH KEY:
- — Backstitch/Straight
- ● French Knot
- ✕ Cross

Overcast edges.

2: Using three strands floss and metallic braid or cord in colors and embroidery stitches indicated, embroider detail as indicated on graph.

3: Hang or display as desired.

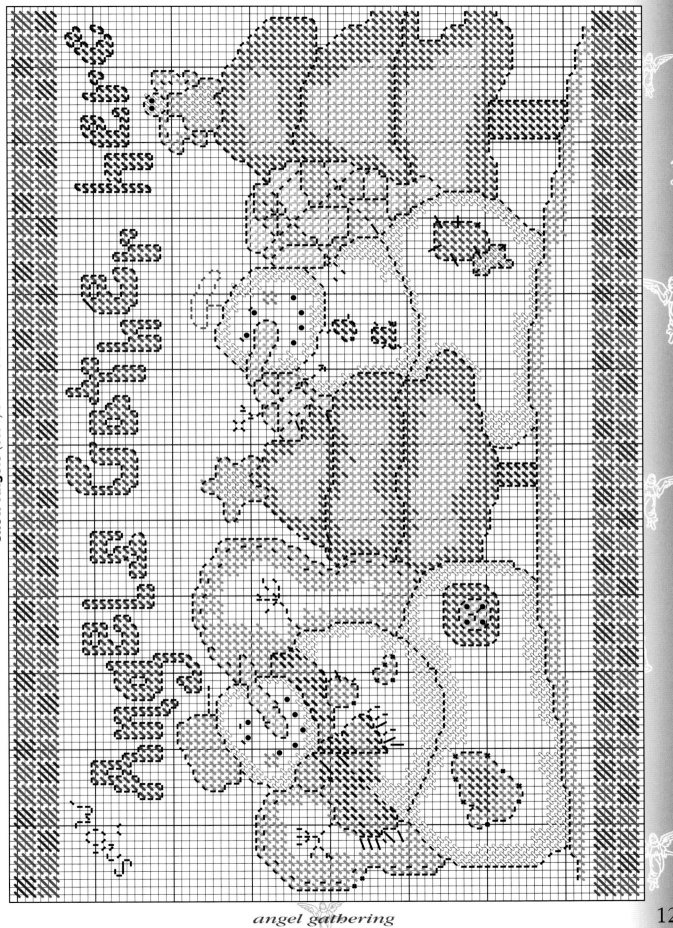

angel gathering

designed by
Darla
Fanton

herald angels
music organizer

skill level & size

Challenging skill level. 6¾" x 10¼" x 6" tall [17.1cm x 26cm x 15.2cm].

materials

- Three sheets of 7-count plastic canvas
- Six-strand embroidery floss; for amounts see Color Key.
- ⅛" [3mm] metallic ribbon or metallic cord; for amount see Color Key.
- #8 metallic braid or metallic thread; for amount see Color Key.
- Worsted-weight or plastic canvas yarn; for amounts see Color Key.

cutting instructions

A: For lid top, cut one 45 x 68 holes.

B: For lid lip sides, cut two 4 x 58 holes (no graph).

C: For lid lip ends, cut two 4 x 35 holes (no graph).

D: For box ends, cut two 37 x 39 holes.

E: For box sides, cut two 37 x 62 holes.

F: For box bottom, cut one 45 x 68 holes.

stitching instructions

1: Using colors and stitches indicated, work A and D-F pieces (leave uncoded areas of F unworked) according to graphs. Omitting attachment edges, fill in uncoded areas of A, D and E pieces and work B and C pieces using navy and Continental Stitch. With metallic ribbon or cord, Overcast edges of A.

2: Using six strands floss, metallic ribbon or cord and metallic braid or thread in colors and embroidery stitches indicated, embroider detail on A, D and E pieces as indicated on graphs.

3: Whipstitch pieces together according to CD Holder Assembly Diagram.

COLOR KEY: Herald Angel's Music Organizer

Embroidery floss		AMOUNT
Blue		¼ yd. [0.2m]
Red		¼ yd. [0.2m]

⅛" metallic ribbon or cord	Kreinik	AMOUNT
Gold	#002HL	40 yds. [36.6m]

Fine metallic braid or thread	Kreinik	AMOUNT
Gold	#002	8 yds. [7.3m]

Worsted-weight	Berella® "4"® by Spinrite®	YARN AMOUNT
Navy	#8965	3½ oz. [99.2g]
White	#8942	9 yds. [8.2m]
Deep Rose	#8923	8 yds. [7.3m]
Light Rose	#8922	3 yds. [2.7m]
Med. Teal	#8844	2½ yds. [2.3m]
Pastel Peach	#8947	1 yd. [0.9m]
Med. Brown	#8796	1 yd. [0.9m]
Pale Antique Rose	#8814	½ yd. [0.5m]

STITCH KEY:

- — Backstitch/Straight
- ● French Knot
- ✕ Cross Stitch
- ⌒ Lazy Daisy
- ☐ Lid Side and End Lip/Top Attachment
- ☐ Side and End/Bottom Attachment

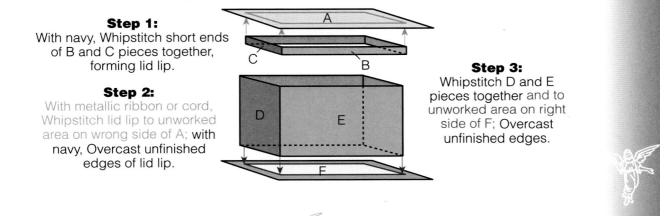

CD Holder Assembly Diagram
(Pieces are shown in different colors for contrast; gray denotes wrong side.)

Step 1:
With navy, Whipstitch short ends of B and C pieces together, forming lid lip.

Step 2:
With metallic ribbon or cord, Whipstitch lid lip to unworked area on wrong side of A; with navy, Overcast unfinished edges of lid lip.

Step 3:
Whipstitch D and E pieces together and to unworked area on right side of F; Overcast unfinished edges.

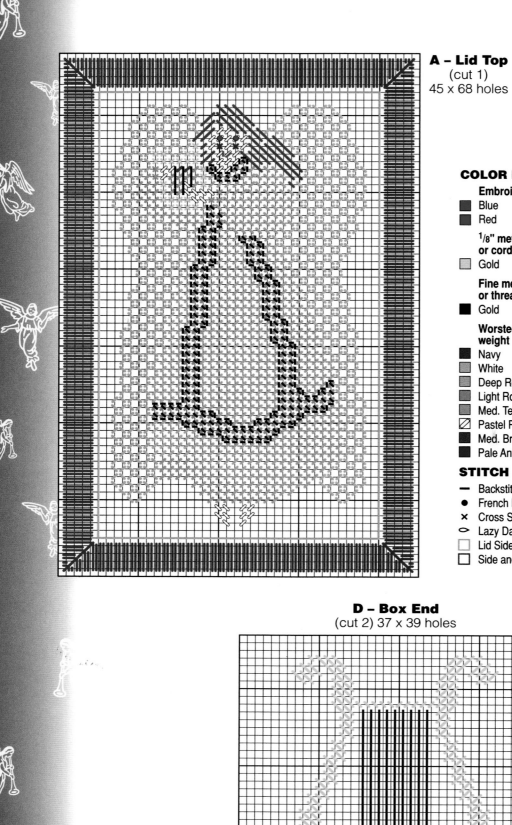

A – Lid Top
(cut 1)
45 x 68 holes

COLOR KEY: Herald Angel's Music Organizer

Embroidery floss		AMOUNT
■ Blue		1/4 yd. [0.2m]
■ Red		1/4 yd. [0.2m]

1/8" metallic ribbon or cord	Kreinik	AMOUNT
■ Gold	#002HL	40 yds. [36.6m]

Fine metallic braid or thread	Kreinik	AMOUNT
■ Gold	#002	8 yds. [7.3m]

Worsted-weight	Berella® "4"® by Spinrite®	YARN AMOUNT
■ Navy	#8965	3 1/2 oz. [99.2g]
■ White	#8942	9 yds. [8.2m]
■ Deep Rose	#8923	8 yds. [7.3m]
■ Light Rose	#8922	3 yds. [2.7m]
■ Med. Teal	#8844	2 1/2 yds. [2.3m]
▨ Pastel Peach	#8947	1 yd. [0.9m]
■ Med. Brown	#8796	1 yd. [0.9m]
■ Pale Antique Rose	#8814	1/2 yd. [0.5m]

STITCH KEY:
- — Backstitch/Straight
- ● French Knot
- × Cross Stitch
- ⌢ Lazy Daisy
- ☐ Lid Side and End Lip/Top Attachment
- ☐ Side and End/Bottom Attachment

D – Box End
(cut 2) 37 x 39 holes

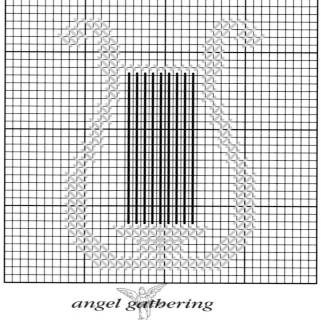

angel gathering

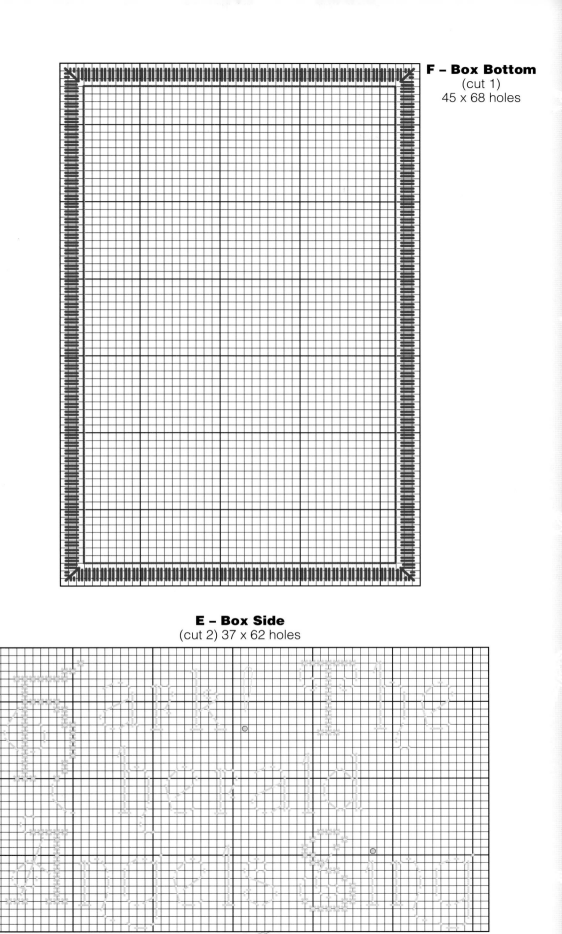

F – Box Bottom
(cut 1)
45 x 68 holes

E – Box Side
(cut 2) 37 x 62 holes

angels over Bethlehem

designed by
Kristine
Loffredo

skill level & size

Challenging skill level. 18" x 19" [45.7cm x 48.3cm].

materials

- Four sheets of 7-count plastic canvas
- Craft glue or glue gun
- Metallic cord; for amounts see individual Color Keys.
- Worsted-weight or plastic canvas yarn; for amounts see individual Color Keys.

cutting instructions

A: For angels #1–#3, cut one each according to graphs.

B: For arms, cut three according to graph.

C: For cloud, cut one according to graph.

D: For buildings #1 and #2, cut one each according to graphs.

stitching instructions

1: Using colors and stitches indicated, work A, one B, C and D (leave uncoded area of D#2 unworked) pieces according to graphs; substituting royal and red for Xmas green, work one remaining B in each color according to graph. Omitting attachment edges, with solid gold for star, white for building sides and tops, gray for cloud and with matching colors as shown in photo, Overcast edges of pieces.

2: Using yarn and in colors and embroidery stitches indicated, embroider detail on A pieces

A – Angel #1
(cut 1) 57 x 58 holes

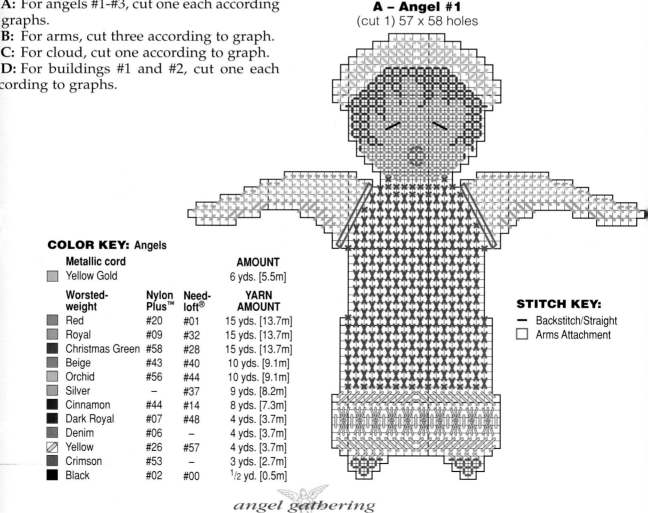

COLOR KEY: Angels

Metallic cord			AMOUNT
Yellow Gold			6 yds. [5.5m]

Worsted-weight	Nylon Plus™	Need-loft®	YARN AMOUNT
Red	#20	#01	15 yds. [13.7m]
Royal	#09	#32	15 yds. [13.7m]
Christmas Green	#58	#28	15 yds. [13.7m]
Beige	#43	#40	10 yds. [9.1m]
Orchid	#56	#44	10 yds. [9.1m]
Silver	–	#37	9 yds. [8.2m]
Cinnamon	#44	#14	8 yds. [7.3m]
Dark Royal	#07	#48	4 yds. [3.7m]
Denim	#06	–	4 yds. [3.7m]
Yellow	#26	#57	4 yds. [3.7m]
Crimson	#53	–	3 yds. [2.7m]
Black	#02	#00	½ yd. [0.5m]

STITCH KEY:
- — Backstitch/Straight
- ☐ Arms Attachment

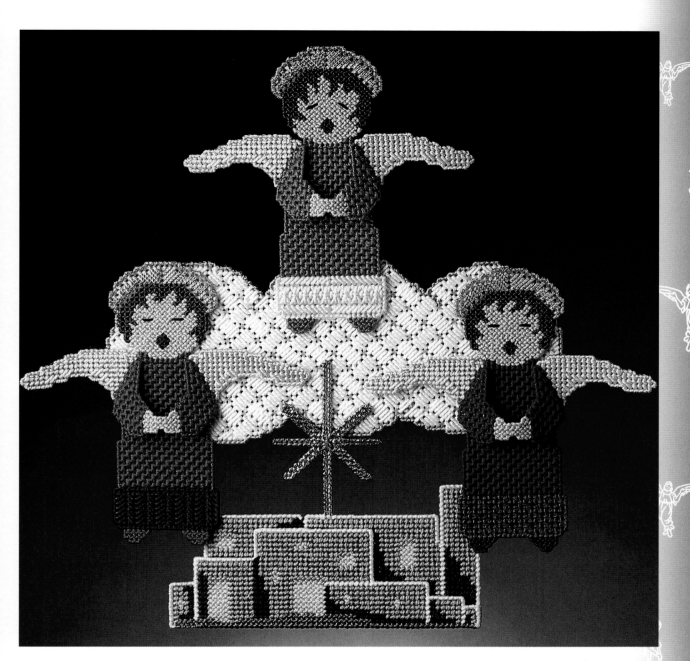

D – Building #1
(cut 1) 20 x 56 holes

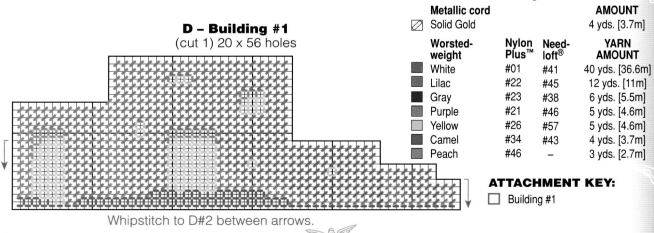

Whipstitch to D#2 between arrows.

COLOR KEY: Buildings & Cloud

Metallic cord			AMOUNT
▨ Solid Gold			4 yds. [3.7m]

Worsted-weight	Nylon Plus™	Need-loft®	YARN AMOUNT
White	#01	#41	40 yds. [36.6m]
Lilac	#22	#45	12 yds. [11m]
Gray	#23	#38	6 yds. [5.5m]
Purple	#21	#46	5 yds. [4.6m]
Yellow	#26	#57	5 yds. [4.6m]
Camel	#34	#43	4 yds. [3.7m]
Peach	#46	–	3 yds. [2.7m]

ATTACHMENT KEY:

☐ Building #1

angel gathering

as indicated on graphs.

3: Holding wrong side of D#1 to unworked area on right side of D#2, with white for sides and camel for bottom, Whipstitch D pieces together as indicated. Glue remaining edges to secure. For each angel, holding one B to right side of corresponding A, with matching colors, Whipstitch together as indicated. (Arms do not lay flat.)

4: Glue star to cloud; glue angels to cloud and buildings as shown or as desired.

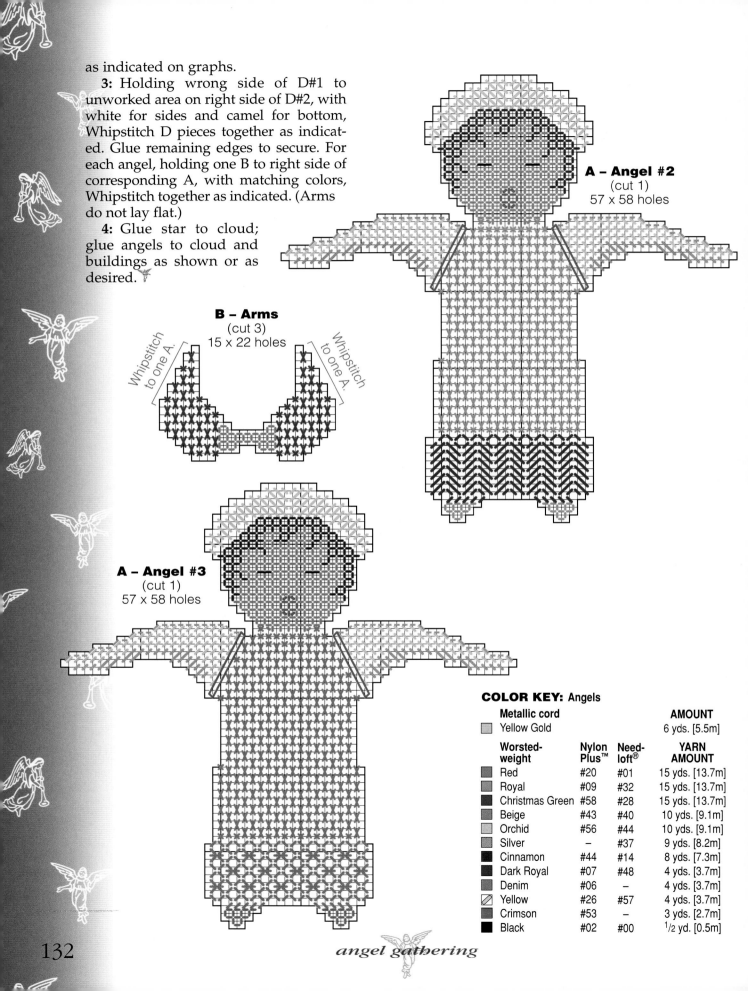

A – Angel #2
(cut 1)
57 x 58 holes

B – Arms
(cut 3)
15 x 22 holes

Whipstitch to one A.

Whipstitch to one A.

A – Angel #3
(cut 1)
57 x 58 holes

COLOR KEY: Angels

	Metallic cord			AMOUNT
	Yellow Gold			6 yds. [5.5m]

	Worsted-weight	Nylon Plus™	Need-loft®	YARN AMOUNT
	Red	#20	#01	15 yds. [13.7m]
	Royal	#09	#32	15 yds. [13.7m]
	Christmas Green	#58	#28	15 yds. [13.7m]
	Beige	#43	#40	10 yds. [9.1m]
	Orchid	#56	#44	10 yds. [9.1m]
	Silver	–	#37	9 yds. [8.2m]
	Cinnamon	#44	#14	8 yds. [7.3m]
	Dark Royal	#07	#48	4 yds. [3.7m]
	Denim	#06	–	4 yds. [3.7m]
	Yellow	#26	#57	4 yds. [3.7m]
	Crimson	#53	–	3 yds. [2.7m]
	Black	#02	#00	1/2 yd. [0.5m]

C – Cloud (cut 1) 39 x 90 holes

COLOR KEY: Buildings & Cloud

Metallic cord			AMOUNT
▨ Solid Gold			4 yds. [3.7m]

Worsted-weight	Nylon Plus™	Need-loft®	YARN AMOUNT
White	#01	#41	40 yds. [36.6m]
Lilac	#22	#45	12 yds. [11m]
Gray	#23	#38	6 yds. [5.5m]
Purple	#21	#46	5 yds. [4.6m]
Yellow	#26	#57	5 yds. [4.6m]
Camel	#34	#43	4 yds. [3.7m]
Peach	#46	–	3 yds. [2.7m]

ATTACHMENT KEY:

☐ Building #1

D – Building #2
(cut 1)
55 x 61 holes

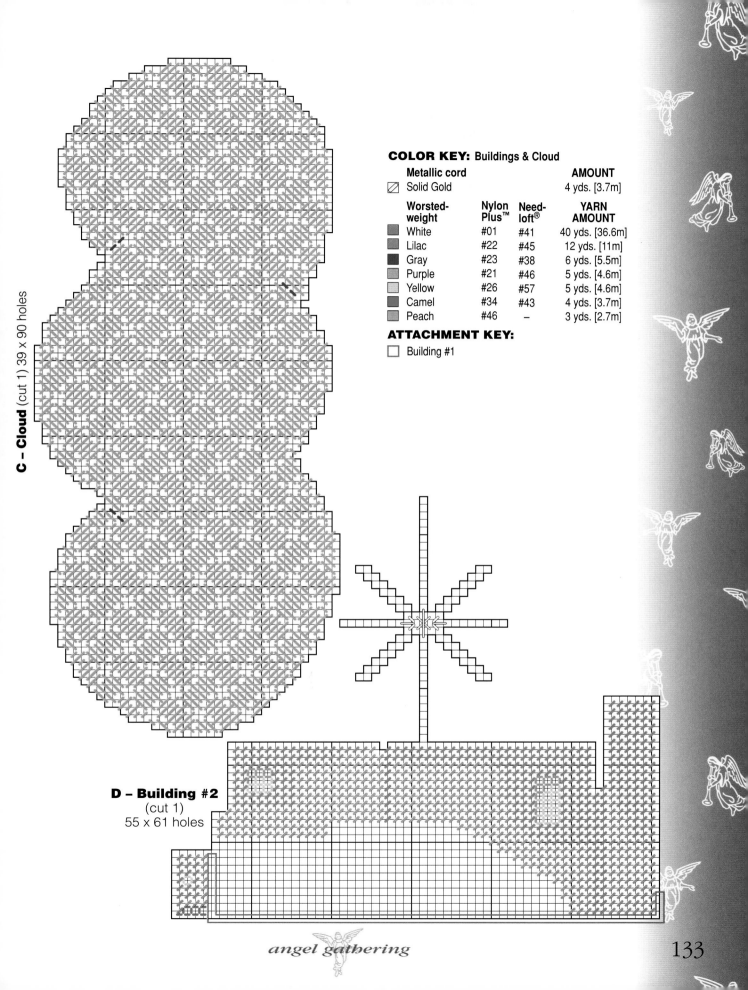

designed by
Janelle Giese of
Janelle Marie Designs

angel bell

skill level & size

Challenging skill level. 3" x 3½" x 7¼" tall [7.6cm x 8.9cm x 18.4cm].

materials

- One sheet of 7-count plastic canvas
- Dark blonde wavy doll hair
- One gold 1" [2.5cm] jingle bell
- 15 Victorian gold glass seed beads
- Beading needle and matching-color thread
- Craft glue or glue gun
- Six-strand embroidery floss; for amount see Color Key.
- #8 perle coton; for amount see Color Key.
- Heavy metallic braid or metallic cord; for amount see Color Key.
- Worsted-weight or plastic canvas yarn; for amounts see Color Key.

cutting instructions

A: For head, cut one according to graph.
B: For dress front and back panels, cut two (one for front and one for back) according to graph.
C: For dress side panels, cut two according to graph.
D: For dress corner panels, cut four according to graph.
E: For dress sleeves, cut one according to graph.
F: For hands, cut one according to graph.
G: For wings, cut one according to graph.
H: For collar, cut one according to graph.

stitching instructions

1: Using colors and stitches indicated, work B-E pieces according to graphs; fill in uncoded areas of B-E pieces are work G and H pieces using white and Continental Stitch. Using peach and Continental Stitch, work A and F pieces. With baby blue for wings and with matching colors as shown in photo, Overcast edges of A, E, G and H pieces.

2: Using yarn (Separate into individual plies,

if desired.), perle coton, floss and braid or cord in colors and embroidery stitches indicated, embroider detail on A (work eye stitches four times; see photo), B-E, G and H pieces as indicated on graphs. With beading needle and thread, sew beads on B, C and H pieces as indicated.

NOTE: Cut one 3" [7.6cm] length of braid or cord.

3: With white, Whipstitch X edges of each B wrong sides together; repeat with each C and with H. Whipstitch and assemble braid or cord, bell and A-H pieces as indicated and according to Angel Bell Assembly Diagram.

NOTE: Cut one 9" [22.9cm] and one 4½" [11.4cm] length of braid or cord.

4: For halo, bend 4½" strand into a circle,

gluing ends to secure; tie 9" strand into a bow and glue to halo.

5: Glue hair around front and to back of head, trimming ends to achieve desired effect; glue halo to back of head.

A – Head
(cut 1)
13 x 26 holes

C – Dress Side Panel
(cut 2) 9 x 31 holes
Whipstitch X edges together.

Whipstitch to one B.

Whipstitch to one B.

Whipstitch to one D.

Whipstitch to one D.

COLOR KEY: Angel Bell

#8 perle coton	DMC®	AMOUNT
■ Black	#310	1/2 yd. [0.5m]

Embroidery floss	DMC®	AMOUNT
▨ 2-strands salmon	#3328	1/2 yd. [0.5m]

Metallic braid or cord	Kreinik	AMOUNT
▨ Vatican	#102HL	5 yds. [4.6m]

Worsted-weight	Nylon Plus™	Need-loft®	YARN AMOUNT
☐ White	#01	#41	28 yds. [25.6m]
▨ Red	#20	#01	8 yds. [7.3m]
☐ Peach	#46	–	3 yds. [2.7m]
▨ Baby Blue	#05	#36	2 yds. [1.8m]
▨ Holly	#31	#27	1 yd. [0.9m]

STITCH KEY:
- — Backstitch/Straight
- ✳ Smyrna Cross
- ✕ Cross
- ○ Bead Attachment
- ✦ Bell Attachment

D – Dress Corner Panel
(cut 4) 5 x 19 holes

Whipstitch to one B or C.

Whipstitch to one B or C.

F – Hands
(cut 1) 3 x 5 holes

Whipstitch to E.

Whipstitch to E.

Angel Bell Assembly Diagram
(Pieces are shown in different colors for contrast; gray denotes wrong side.)

Step 1:
Thread 3" braid or cord strand through ✦ hole on A (shown in outline form for clarity) and through top of bell; tie ends into a knot.

A

B

C

C

D

D

B

Bell

Step 2:
Holding B and C pieces wrong sides together with A between, Whipstitch together, attaching one D at each corner as you work.

Step 3:
With red, Overcast unfinished bottom edges of dress

A

G

H

F

E

Dress Assembly

Step 4:
Glue wrong side of E to back of Dress Assembly.

Step 5:
Bend sleeve cuffs of E around to front and with peach, Whipstitch E and F pieces together; Overcast edges of F.

Step 5:
Place H around head and glue to secure; glue G to dress back.

angel gathering

135

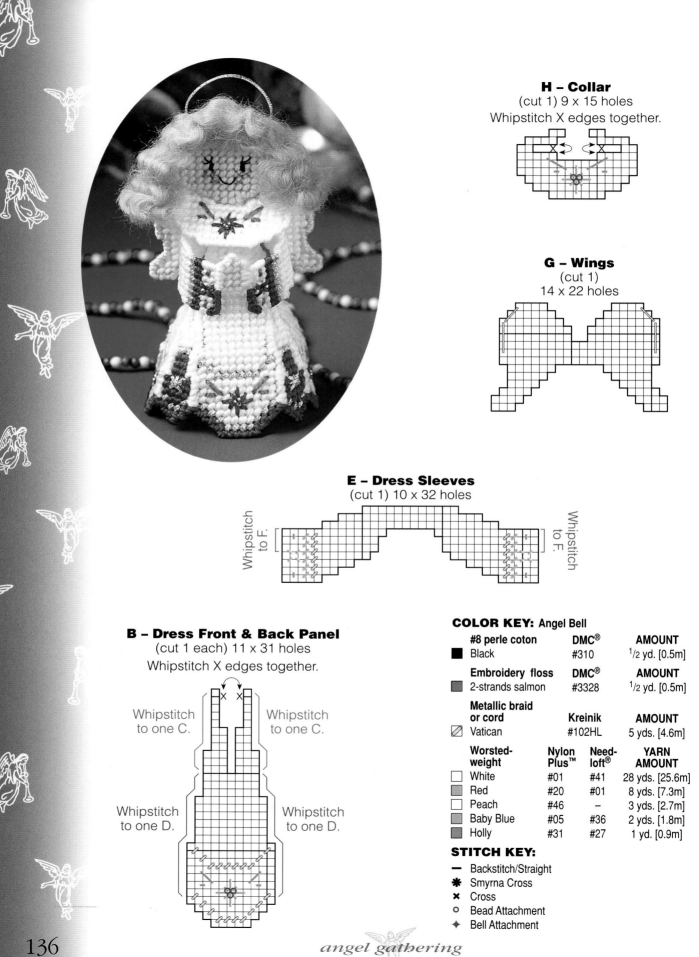

H – Collar
(cut 1) 9 x 15 holes
Whipstitch X edges together.

G – Wings
(cut 1)
14 x 22 holes

E – Dress Sleeves
(cut 1) 10 x 32 holes

Whipstitch to F.

Whipstitch to F.

B – Dress Front & Back Panel
(cut 1 each) 11 x 31 holes
Whipstitch X edges together.

Whipstitch to one C.

Whipstitch to one C.

Whipstitch to one D.

Whipstitch to one D.

COLOR KEY: Angel Bell

#8 perle coton	DMC®	AMOUNT
■ Black	#310	1/2 yd. [0.5m]

Embroidery floss	DMC®	AMOUNT
■ 2-strands salmon	#3328	1/2 yd. [0.5m]

Metallic braid or cord	Kreinik	AMOUNT
▨ Vatican	#102HL	5 yds. [4.6m]

Worsted-weight	Nylon Plus™	Need-loft®	YARN AMOUNT
□ White	#01	#41	28 yds. [25.6m]
▨ Red	#20	#01	8 yds. [7.3m]
□ Peach	#46	–	3 yds. [2.7m]
▨ Baby Blue	#05	#36	2 yds. [1.8m]
▨ Holly	#31	#27	1 yd. [0.9m]

STITCH KEY:
- — Backstitch/Straight
- ✳ Smyrna Cross
- ✕ Cross
- ○ Bead Attachment
- ✦ Bell Attachment

angel gathering

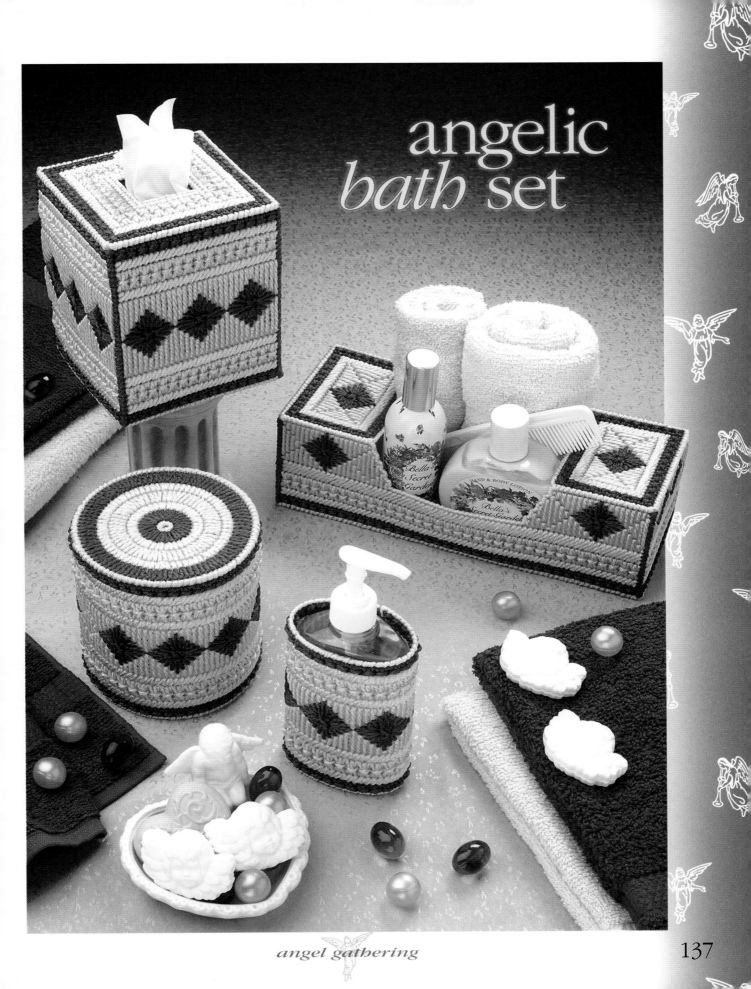

angelic
bath set

designed by
Joyce
Horovitz

angelic bath set

skill level & size

Average skill level. Tissue Cover loosely covers a boutique-style tissue box; Liquid Soap Dispenser Cover snugly covers a 7.5 fl. oz. liquid soap container; Towel Holder is 4¼" x 11¼" x 3½" tall [10.8cm x 28.6cm x 8.9cm]; Toilet Tissue Cover conceals a standard-size roll of toilet tissue.

materials

- One 12" x 18" [30.5cm x 45.7cm] or larger and three standard-size sheets of 7-count plastic canvas
- One 6" [15.2cm] plastic canvas radial circle
- Velcro® closure (optional)
- Worsted-weight or plastic canvas yarn; for amounts see Color Key.

cutting instructions

A: For Tissue Cover top, cut one according to graph.

B: For Tissue Cover sides, cut four 31 x 37 holes.

C: For Tissue Cover optional bottom and flap, cut one 31 x 31 holes for bottom and one 12 x 31 holes for flap (no graphs).

D: For Liquid Soap Dispenser Cover, cut one 33 x 53 holes.

E: For Towel Holder ends, cut two 22 x 27 holes.

F: For Towel Holder sides, cut two according to graph.

G: For Towel Holder top pieces, cut two 19 x 27 holes.

H: For Towel Holder bottom, cut one 27 x 73 holes (no graph).

I: For Toilet Tissue Cover top, cut one from 6" circle according to graph.

J: For Toilet Tissue Cover side, cut one 33 x 99 holes.

stitching instructions

NOTE: C and H pieces are not worked.

1: Using colors and stitches indicated, work A, B, D-G, I and J (overlap ends as indicated on graphs and work through both thicknesses at overlap area to join) pieces according to graphs. With silver, Overcast cutout edges of A.

2: For Tissue Cover, with burgundy, Whipstitch long edges of B pieces together, forming side assembly. With silver, Whipstitch A to side assembly, forming Cover. For optional bottom, Whipstitch C pieces together and to one Cover side according to Optional Tissue Cover Bottom Assembly Illustration; Overcast unfinished edges of Cover. If desired, glue closure to flap and inside of Cover.

3: For Liquid Soap Dispenser Cover, with burgundy, Whipstitch short ends of D wrong sides together; with silver, Overcast unfinished edges.

4: Whipstitch E-H pieces together according to Towel Holder Assembly Diagram.

5: For Toilet Tissue Cover, with silver, Whipstitch I and J pieces wrong sides together; Overcast unfinished edges.

Towel Holder Assembly Diagram
(Pieces are shown in different colors for contrast; gray denotes wrong side.)

Step 1:
With burgundy, Whipstitch E and F pieces together, forming side assembly.

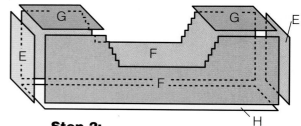

Step 2:
With silver, Whipstitch G and H pieces to side assembly.

Step 3:
Overcast unfinished edges.

A – Tissue Cover Top
(cut 1) 31 x 31 holes

B – Tissue Cover Side
(cut 4) 31 x 37 holes

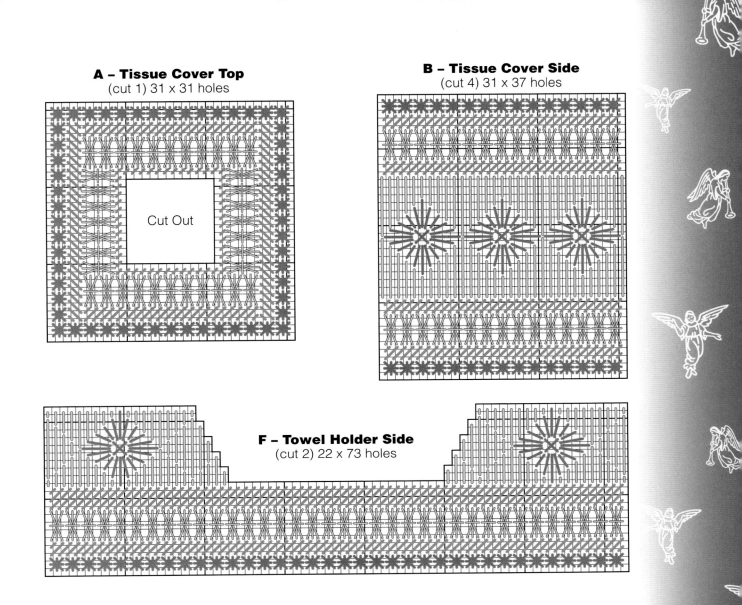

Cut Out

F – Towel Holder Side
(cut 2) 22 x 73 holes

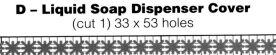

COLOR KEY: Angelic Bath Set

Worsted-weight	Nylon Plus™	Need-loft®	YARN AMOUNT
Burgundy	#13	#03	2¹/₂ oz. [70.9g]
Pink	#11	#07	2¹/₂ oz. [70.9g]
Silver	–	#37	2¹/₂ oz. [70.9g]

D – Liquid Soap Dispenser Cover
(cut 1) 33 x 53 holes

Optional Tissue Cover Bottom Assembly Illustration

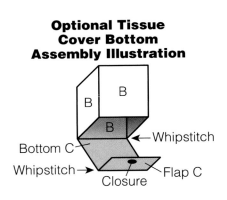

B

B

B

Whipstitch

Bottom C

Whipstitch

Flap C

Closure

angel gathering

E – Towel Holder End
(cut 2) 22 x 27 holes

I – Toilet Tissue Holder Top
(use 6" circle)
Cut away gray areas.

G – Towel Holder Top Piece
(cut 2) 19 x 27 holes

COLOR KEY: Angelic Bath Set

	Worsted-weight	Nylon Plus™	Need-loft®	YARN AMOUNT
■	Burgundy	#13	#03	2¹/₂ oz. [70.9g]
▨	Pink	#11	#07	2¹/₂ oz. [70.9g]
▨	Silver	–	#37	2¹/₂ oz. [70.9g]

Lap
Under

J – Toilet Tissue Cover Side
(cut 1 from large sheet) 33 x 99 holes

Lap
Over

Continue established pattern
across unseen area.

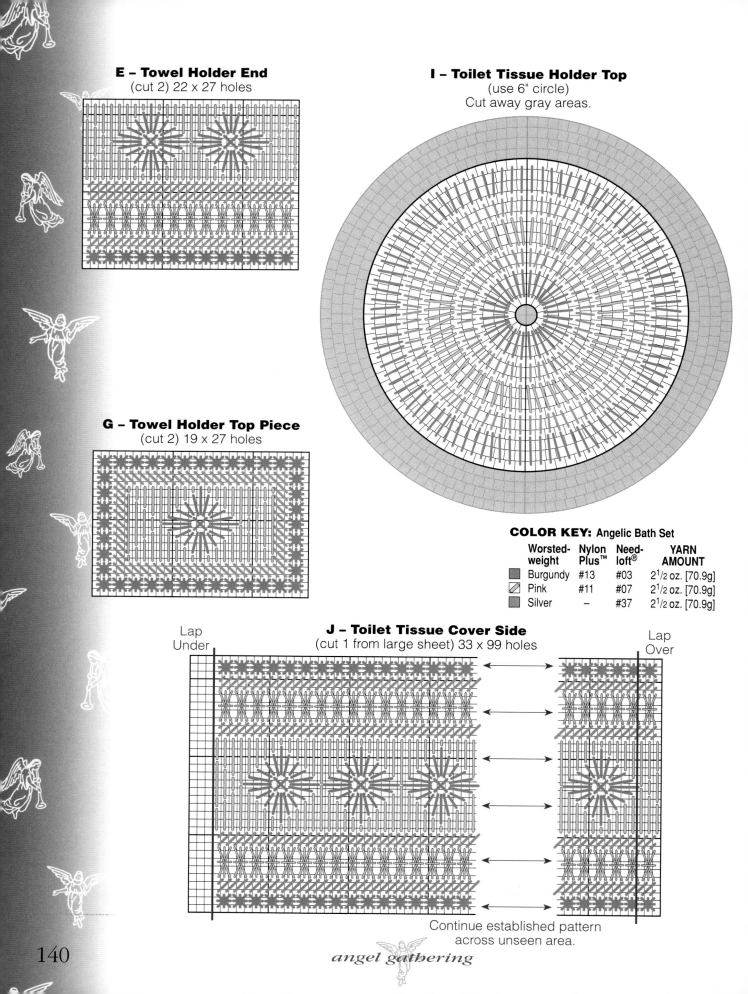

angel gathering

angel bear frame & door hanger

designed by
Kimberly A.
Suber

angel bear frame & door hanger

skill level & size

Average skill level. Frame is 7" x 10" [17.8cm x 25.4cm] with a 3¾" x 4¾" [9.5cm x 12.1cm] photo window; Door Hanger is 5¼" x 10⅛" [13.3cm x 25.7cm].

materials

- Four sheets of 7-count plastic canvas
- Three of each red and green 10mm round acrylic stones
- Craft glue or glue gun
- Heavy metallic cord; for amounts see Color Key.
- Worsted-weight or plastic canvas yarn; for amounts see Color Key.

cutting instructions

A: For Frame, cut one according to graph.
B: For Door Hanger, cut one according to graph.
C: For white and brown bear, cut one each according to graphs.
D: For wings, cut four according to graph.

stitching instructions

1: Using colors and stitches indicated, work pieces (two D on opposite side of canvas) according to graphs; with yellow gold for cut-out edges of Frame and Door Hanger and with matching colors as shown in photo, Overcast edges of pieces.

2: Using black and Backstitch, embroider detail on C pieces as indicated on graphs. Glue

COLOR KEY: Angel Bear Frame & Door Hanger

Metallic cord			AMOUNT
Yellow Gold			12 yds. [11m]
Solid Gold			4 yds. [3.7m]

Worsted-weight	Nylon Plus™	Need-loft®	YARN AMOUNT
Holly	#31	#27	60 yds. [54.9m]
Red	#20	#01	50 yds. [45.7m]
Rust	#51	#09	6 yds. [5.5m]
White	#01	#41	6 yds. [5.5m]
Eggshell	#24	#39	4 yds. [3.7m]
Black	#02	#00	1 yd. [0.9m]
Beige	#43	#40	½ yd. [0.5m]
Gray	#23	#38	½ yd. [0.5m]
Pink	#11	#07	½ yd. [0.5m]

STITCH KEY:
— Backstitch/Straight

B – Door Hanger
(cut 1) 34 x 67 holes

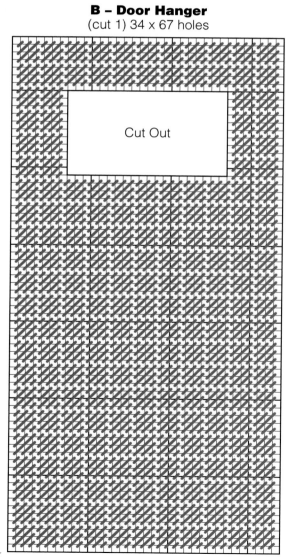

Cut Out

green stones to white bear and red stones to brown bear as shown in photo; glue two wings to wrong side of each bear as shown.

NOTE: Cut two 3" [7.6cm] lengths of solid gold cord.

3: For halos, glue ends of one cord length to wrong side of each bear's heads; glue white bear to Frame and brown bear to Door Hanger as shown. Glue photo to wrong side of Frame cutout.

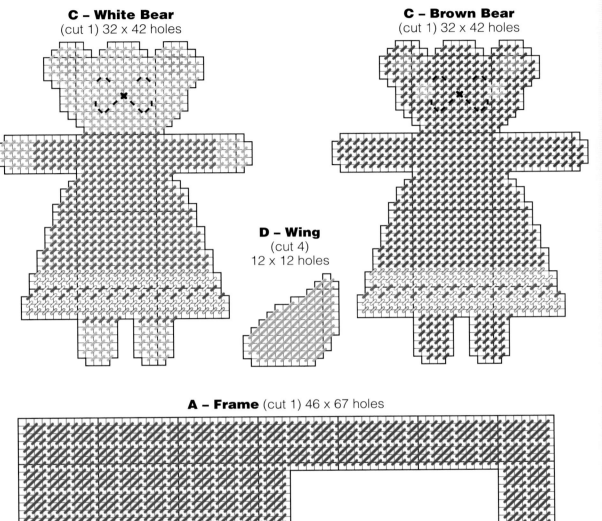

C – White Bear
(cut 1) 32 x 42 holes

C – Brown Bear
(cut 1) 32 x 42 holes

D – Wing
(cut 4)
12 x 12 holes

A – Frame (cut 1) 46 x 67 holes

Cut Out

angel gathering

designed by
**Sandi
Tucker**

angel *tree* topper

skill level & size

Challenging skill level. Fits over an 11½" tall [29.2cm] fashion doll.

materials

- Five sheets of 14-count plastic canvas
- 11½" tall [29.2cm] fashion doll
- 45 silver 4mm beads
- 24 gold 6mm beads
- 187 aurora borealis E beads
- Beading needle, sewing needle and white sewing thread
- Four white marabou craft feathers
- Craft glue or glue gun
- 1 yd. [0.9m] of 1" [2.5cm] gold/white pre-gathered lace
- Medium metallic braid or metallic cord; for amount see Color Key on page 146.
- Six-strand embroidery floss; for amounts see Color Key.

cutting instructions

A: For bodice, cut one according to graph.

B: For bodice sides #1 and #2, cut one each according to graphs.

C: For skirt front, cut one according to graph.

D: For skirt back, cut one according to graph.

E: For wing #1, cut according to Wing #1 Stitch Pattern Guide and Cutting Guide.

F: For wings #2-#4, cut number indicated according to graphs.

G: For halo, cut one according to graph.

H: For sash, cut one according to graph.

stitching instructions

1: Using colors and stitches indicated, work A-H (one of each F on opposite side of canvas) pieces according to graphs, Overcast edges of A-H pieces. With pearl for wing #1, white for wings #2-#4 and with indicated and matching colors, Overcast edges of A-H pieces.

2: Using metallic gold floss and embroidery stitches indicated, embroider detail on A, C, D and H pieces as indicated on graphs.

3: With beading needle and white thread, sew beads to C, D, G and H pieces as indicated.

NOTE: Cut one 24" [61cm] and three 4" [10.2cm] pieces of lace.

4: With sewing needle and white thread, sew A-D pieces wrong sides together as indicated and according to Dress Assembly Diagram. Glue 24" piece of lace to wrong side of skirt bottom, one 4" piece of lace around waist and one 4" piece of lace around each armhole (see photo), trimming away excess as needed to fit.

5: Cut and bend craft feathers, gluing around top edges on wrong side of wing #1; glue to secure. Glue E pieces together according to Wing Assembly Illustration; glue wing assembly to back of doll. Glue sash to front of doll and halo to head as shown in photo.

Dress Assembly Diagram
(Pieces are shown in different colors for contrast; gray denotes wrong side. Doll not shown for clarity.)

Step 1:
Sew C and D pieces wrong sides together, forming skirt.

Step 2:
Place skirt on doll; overlap and sew top back edges closed to achieve a snug fit around doll's waist.

Step 3:
Omitting back seam, sew A and B pieces together, forming bodice.

Step 4:
Place bodice on doll and sew back seam closed.

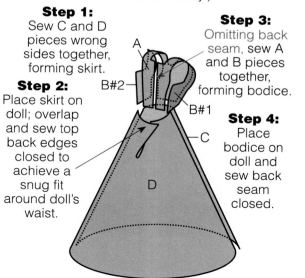

angel gathering

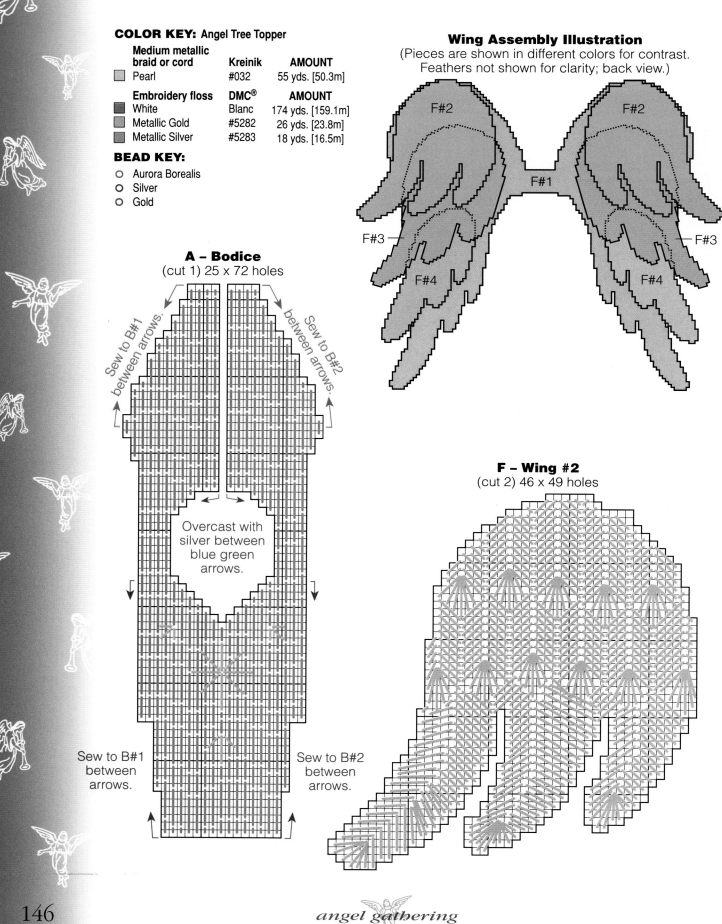

COLOR KEY: Angel Tree Topper

Medium metallic braid or cord	Kreinik	AMOUNT
☐ Pearl	#032	55 yds. [50.3m]

Embroidery floss	DMC®	AMOUNT
■ White	Blanc	174 yds. [159.1m]
▨ Metallic Gold	#5282	26 yds. [23.8m]
▨ Metallic Silver	#5283	18 yds. [16.5m]

BEAD KEY:
- ○ Aurora Borealis
- ○ Silver
- ○ Gold

Wing Assembly Illustration
(Pieces are shown in different colors for contrast. Feathers not shown for clarity; back view.)

F#2 F#2 F#1 F#3 F#3 F#4 F#4

A – Bodice
(cut 1) 25 x 72 holes

Sew to B#1 between arrows.

Sew to B#2 between arrows.

Overcast with silver between blue green arrows.

Sew to B#1 between arrows.

Sew to B#2 between arrows.

F – Wing #2
(cut 2) 46 x 49 holes

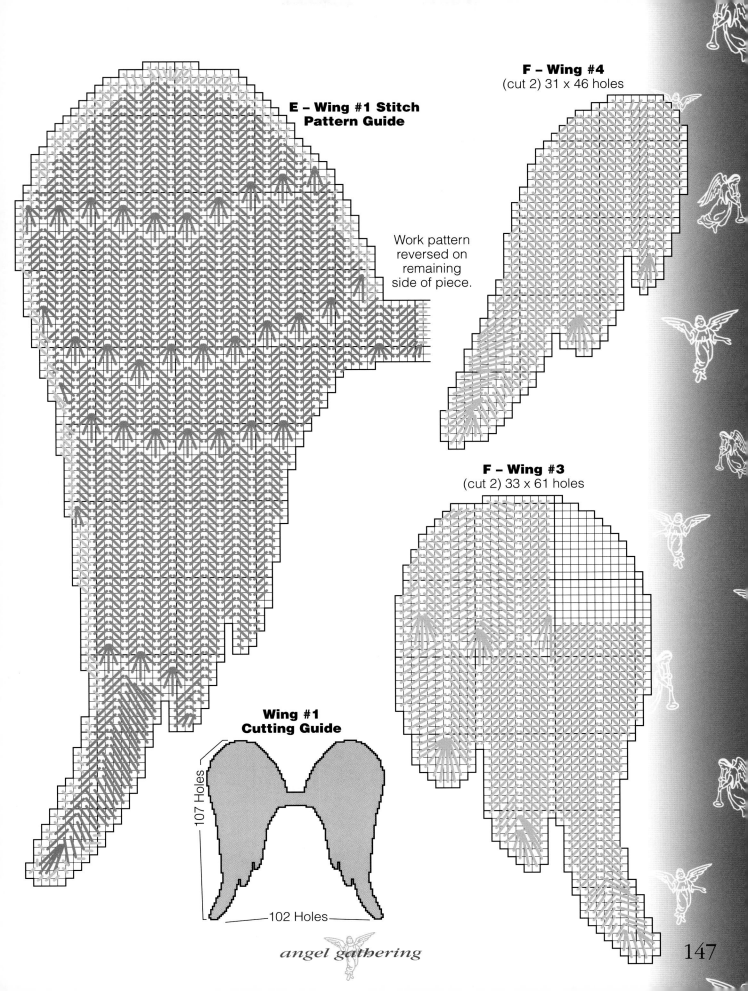

E – Wing #1 Stitch Pattern Guide

F – Wing #4
(cut 2) 31 x 46 holes

Work pattern reversed on remaining side of piece.

F – Wing #3
(cut 2) 33 x 61 holes

Wing #1 Cutting Guide

107 Holes

102 Holes

angel gathering

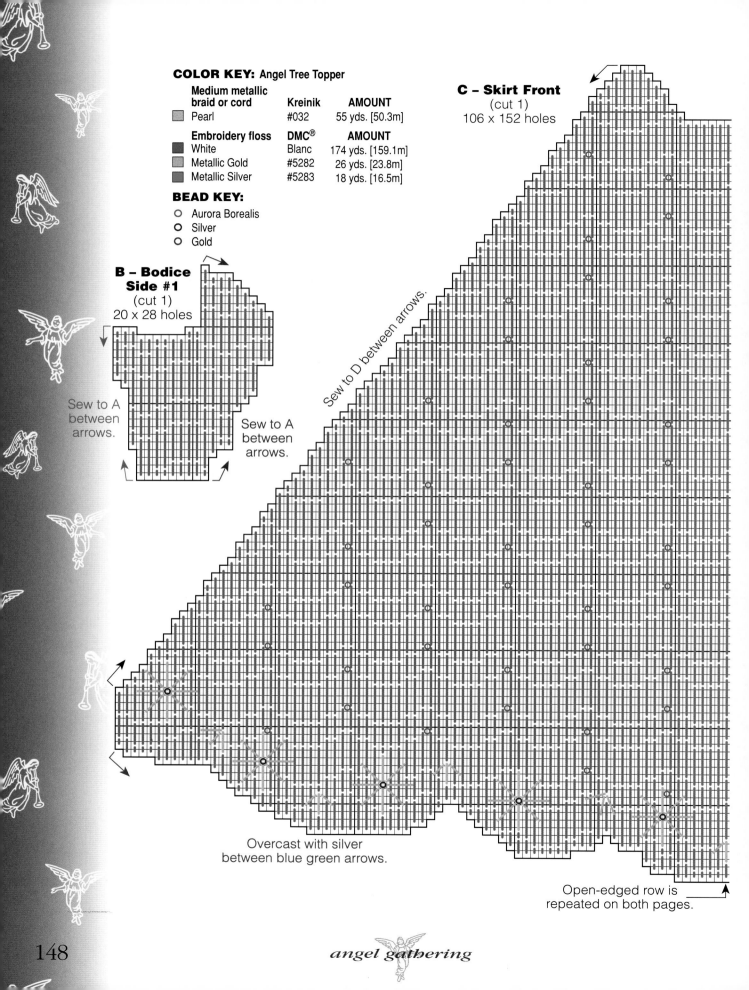

COLOR KEY: Angel Tree Topper

Medium metallic braid or cord

		Kreinik	AMOUNT
	Pearl	#032	55 yds. [50.3m]

Embroidery floss

		DMC®	AMOUNT
	White	Blanc	174 yds. [159.1m]
	Metallic Gold	#5282	26 yds. [23.8m]
	Metallic Silver	#5283	18 yds. [16.5m]

BEAD KEY:

- ○ Aurora Borealis
- ◉ Silver
- ○ Gold

B – Bodice Side #1
(cut 1)
20 x 28 holes

Sew to A between arrows.

Sew to A between arrows.

C – Skirt Front
(cut 1)
106 x 152 holes

Sew to D between arrows.

Overcast with silver between blue green arrows.

Open-edged row is repeated on both pages.

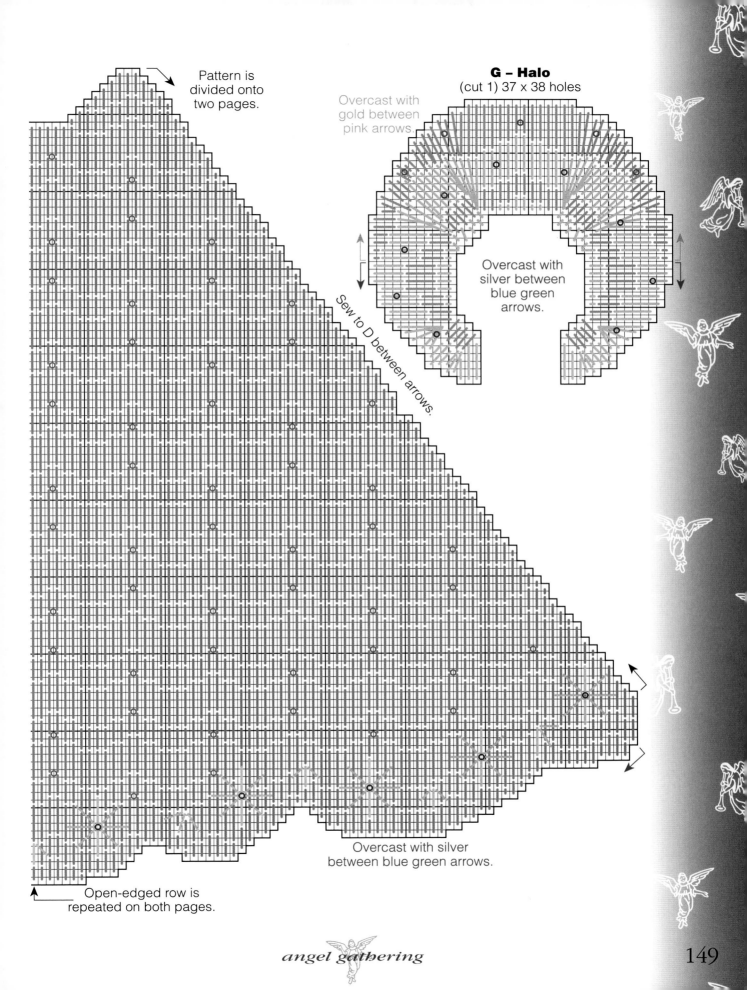

Pattern is divided onto two pages.

G – Halo
(cut 1) 37 x 38 holes

Overcast with gold between pink arrows.

Overcast with silver between blue green arrows.

Sew to D between arrows.

Overcast with silver between blue green arrows.

Open-edged row is repeated on both pages.

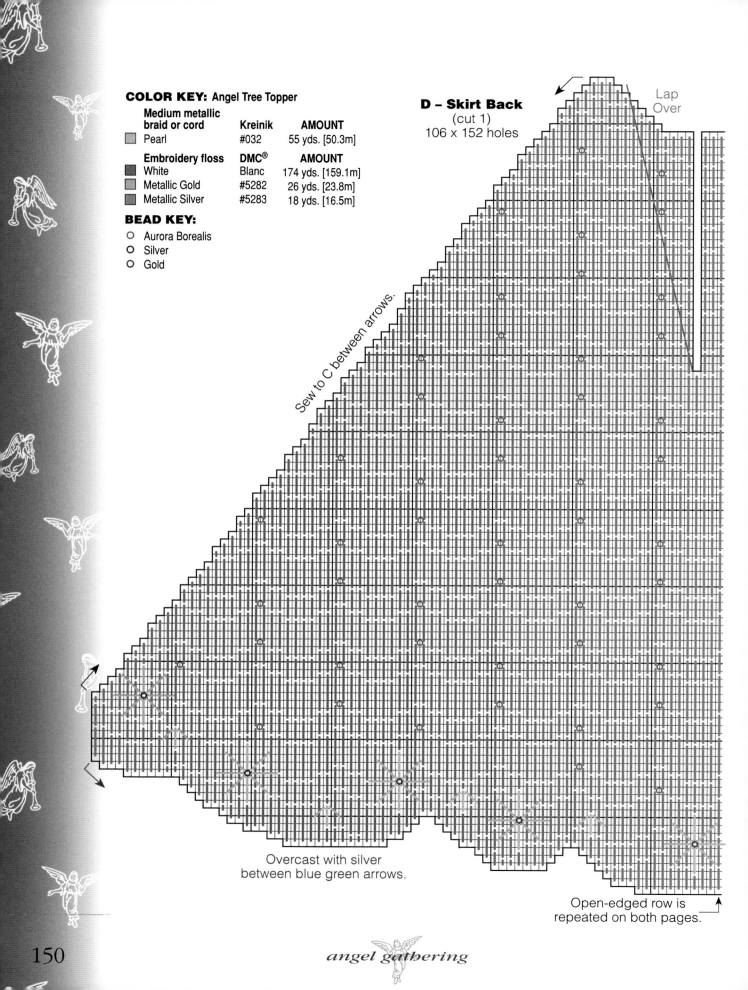

COLOR KEY: Angel Tree Topper

	Medium metallic braid or cord	Kreinik	AMOUNT
☐	Pearl	#032	55 yds. [50.3m]

	Embroidery floss	DMC®	AMOUNT
■	White	Blanc	174 yds. [159.1m]
☐	Metallic Gold	#5282	26 yds. [23.8m]
■	Metallic Silver	#5283	18 yds. [16.5m]

BEAD KEY:

○ Aurora Borealis
○ Silver
○ Gold

D – Skirt Back
(cut 1)
106 x 152 holes

Lap Over

Sew to C between arrows.

Overcast with silver between blue green arrows.

Open-edged row is repeated on both pages.

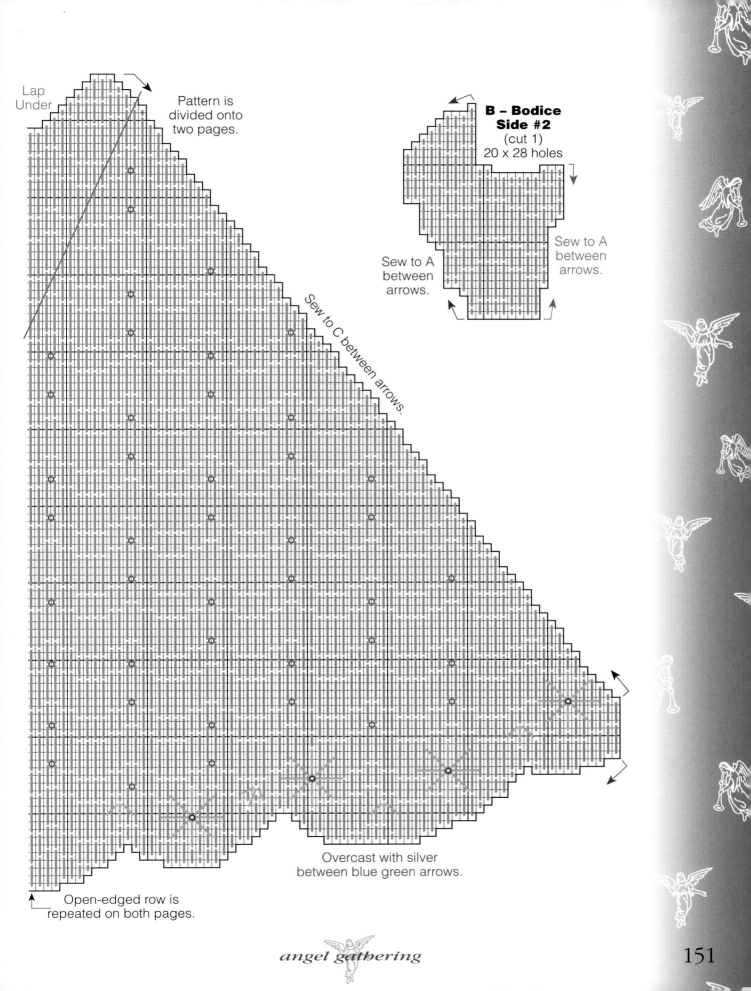

Lap Under

Pattern is divided onto two pages.

Sew to C between arrows.

B – Bodice Side #2
(cut 1)
20 x 28 holes

Sew to A between arrows.

Sew to A between arrows.

Overcast with silver between blue green arrows.

Open-edged row is repeated on both pages.

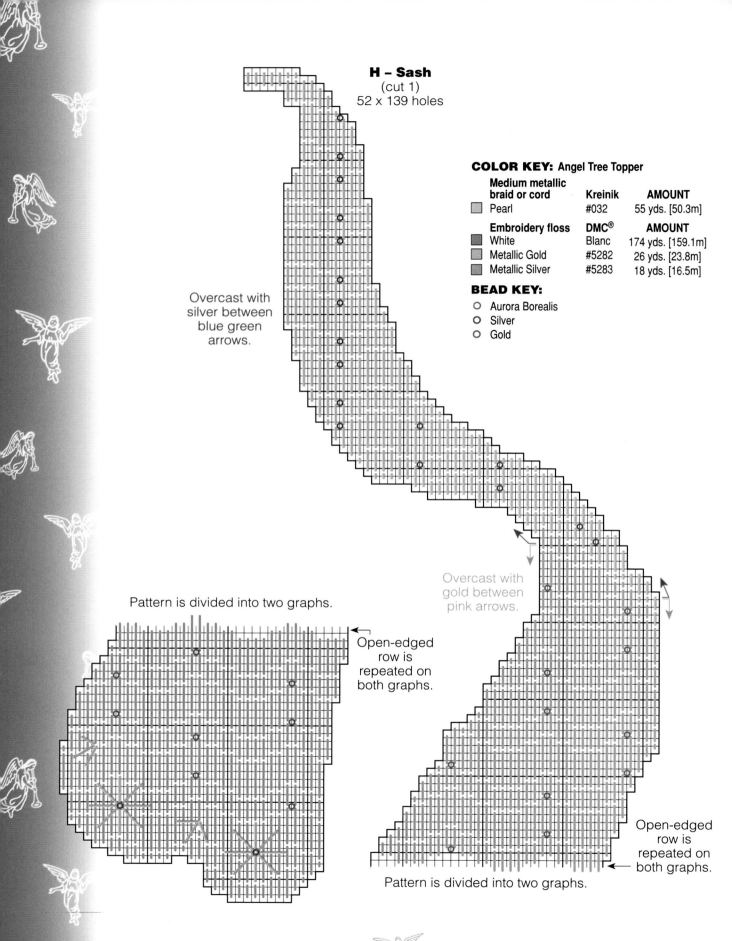

H – Sash
(cut 1)
52 x 139 holes

COLOR KEY: Angel Tree Topper

Medium metallic braid or cord	Kreinik	AMOUNT
Pearl	#032	55 yds. [50.3m]

Embroidery floss	DMC®	AMOUNT
White	Blanc	174 yds. [159.1m]
Metallic Gold	#5282	26 yds. [23.8m]
Metallic Silver	#5283	18 yds. [16.5m]

BEAD KEY:
- Aurora Borealis
- Silver
- Gold

Overcast with silver between blue green arrows.

Overcast with gold between pink arrows.

Pattern is divided into two graphs.

Open-edged row is repeated on both graphs.

Open-edged row is repeated on both graphs.

Pattern is divided into two graphs.

ready, set, *stitch*

getting started

Most plastic canvas stitchers love getting their projects organized before they even step out the door in search of supplies. A few moments of careful planning can make the creation of your project even more fun.

First of all, prepare your work area. You will need a flat surface for cutting and assembly, and you will need a place to store your materials. Good lighting is essential, and a comfortable chair will make your stitching time even more enjoyable.

Do you plan to make one project, or will you be making several of the same item? A materials list appears at the beginning of each pattern. If you plan to make several of the same item, multiply your materials accordingly. Your shopping list is ready.

choosing canvas

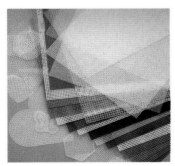

Most projects can be made using standard-size sheets of canvas. Standard size sheets of 7-count (7 holes per inch) are always 70 x 90 holes and are about 10½" x 13½" [26.7cm x 34.3cm]. For larger projects, 7-count canvas also comes in 12" x 18" [30.5cm x 45.7cm], which is always 80 x 120 holes and 13½" x 22½" [34.3cm x 57.2cm], which is always 90 x 150 holes. Other shapes are available in 7-count, including circles, diamonds, purse forms and ovals.

10-count canvas (10 holes per inch) comes only in standard-size sheets, which vary slightly depending on brand. They are 10½" x 13½" [26.7cm x 34.3cm], which is always 106 x 136 holes or 11" x 14" [27.9cm x 35.6cm], which is always 108 x 138 holes.

5-count canvas (5 holes per inch) and 14-count (14 holes per inch) sheets are also available.

Some canvas is soft and pliable, while other canvas is stiffer and more rigid. To prevent canvas from cracking during or after stitching, you'll want to choose pliable canvas for projects that require shaping, like round baskets with curved handles. For easier shaping, warm canvas pieces with a blow-dry hair dryer to soften; dip in cool water to set. If your project is a box or an item that will stand alone, stiffer canvas is more suitable.

Both 7- and 10-count canvas sheets are available in a rainbow of colors. Most designs can be stitched on colored as well as clear canvas. When a pattern does not specify color in the materials list, you can assume clear canvas was used in the photographed model. If you'd like to stitch only a portion of the design, leaving a portion unstitched, use colored canvas to coordinate with yarn colors.

Buy the same brand of canvas for each entire project. Different brands of canvas may differ slightly in the distance between each bar.

marking & counting tools

To avoid wasting canvas, careful cutting of each piece is important. For some pieces with square corners, you might be comfortable cutting the canvas without marking it beforehand. But for pieces with lots of angles and cutouts, you may want to mark your canvas before cutting.

Always count before you mark and cut. To count holes on the graphs, look for the bolder lines showing each ten holes. These ten-count lines begin in the lower left-hand corner of each graph and are on the graph to make counting easier. To count holes on the canvas, you may use your tapestry needle, a toothpick or a plastic hair roller pick. Insert the needle or pick slightly in each hole as you count.

Most stitchers have tried a variety of marking tools and have settled on a favorite, which may be crayon, permanent marker, grease pencil or ball point pen. One of the best marking tools is a fine-point overhead projection marker, available at office supply stores. The ink is dark and easy to see and washes off completely with water. After cutting and before stitching, it's important to remove all marks so they won't stain yarn as you stitch or show through stitches later. Cloth and paper toweling removes grease pencil and crayon marks, as do fabric softener sheets that have already been used in your dryer.

cutting tools

You may find it very helpful to have several tools on hand for cutting canvas. When cutting long, straight sections, scissors, craft cutters or kitchen shears are the fastest and easiest to use. For cutting out detailed areas and trimming nubs, you may like using manicure scissors or nail clippers. If you prefer laying your canvas flat when cutting, try a craft knife and cutting surface – self-healing mats designed for sewing and kitchen cutting boards work well.

stitching materials

You may choose two-ply nylon plastic canvas yarn or four-ply worsted-weight yarn for stitching on 7-count canvas. There are about 42 yards per ounce of plastic canvas yarn and 50 yards per ounce of worsted-weight yarn.

Worsted-weight yarn is widely available and comes in wool, acrylic, cotton and blends. If you decide to use worsted-weight yarn, choose 100% acrylic for best coverage. Select worsted-weight yarn by color instead of the color names or numbers found in the Color Keys. Projects stitched with worsted-weight yarn often "fuzz" after use. "Fuzz" can be removed by shaving it off with a fabric shaver to make your project look new again.

Plastic canvas yarn comes in about 60 colors and is a favorite of many plastic canvas designers. These yarns "wear" well both while stitching and in the finished product. When buying plastic canvas yarn, shop using the color names or numbers found in the Color Keys, or select colors of your choice.

To cover 5-count canvas, use a doubled strand of worsted-weight or plastic canvas yarn.

Choose sport-weight yarn or #3 pearl cotton for stitching on 10-count canvas. To cover 10-count canvas using six-strand embroidery floss, use 12 strands held together. Single

and double plies of yarn will also cover 10-count and can be used for embroidery or accent stitching worked over needlepoint stitches – simply separate worsted-weight yarn into 2-ply or plastic canvas

yarn into 1-ply. Nylon plastic canvas yarn does not perform as well as knitting worsted when separated and can be frustrating to use, but it is possible. Just use short lengths, separate into single plies and twist each ply slightly.

Embroidery floss or #5 pearl cotton can also be used for embroidery, and each covers 14-count canvas well.

Metallic cord is a tightly-woven cord that comes in dozens of glittering colors. Some are solid-color metallics, including gold and silver, and some have colors interwoven with gold or silver threads. If your metallic cord has a white core, the core may be removed for super-easy stitching. To do so, cut a length of cord; grasp center core fibers with tweezers or fingertips and pull. Core slips out easily. Though the sparkly look of metallics will add much to your project, you may substitute contrasting colors of yarn.

Natural and synthetic raffia straw will cover 7-count canvas if flattened before stitching. Use short lengths to prevent splitting, and glue ends to prevent unraveling.

cutting canvas

Follow all Cutting Instructions, Notes and labels above graphs to cut canvas. Each piece is labeled with a letter of the alphabet. Square-sided pieces are cut according to hole count, and some may not have a graph.

Unlike sewing patterns, graphs are not designed to be used as actual patterns but rather as counting, cutting and stitching guides. Therefore, graphs may not be actual size. Count the holes on the graph (see Marking & Counting Tools on page 153), mark your canvas to match, then cut. The old carpenters' adage – "Measure twice, cut once" – is good advice. Trim off the nubs close to the bar, and trim all corners diagonally.

For large projects, as you cut each piece, it is a good idea to label it with its letter and name. Use sticky labels, or fasten scrap paper notes through the canvas with a twist tie or a quick stitch with a scrap of yarn. To stay organized, you many want to store corresponding pieces together in zip-close bags.

If you want to make several of a favorite design to give as gifts or sell at bazaars, make cutting canvas easier and faster by making a master pattern. From colored canvas, cut out one of each piece required. For duplicates, place the colored canvas on top of clear canvas and cut out. If needed, secure the canvas pieces together with paper fasteners, twist ties or yarn. By using this method, you only have to count from the graphs once.

If you accidentally cut or tear a bar or two on your canvas, don't worry! Boo-boos can usually be repaired in one of several ways: heat the tip of a metal skewer and melt the canvas back together; glue torn bars with a tiny drop of craft glue, super glue or hot glue; or reinforce the torn section with a separate piece of canvas placed at the back of your work. When reinforcing with extra canvas, stitch through both thicknesses.

supplies

Yarn, canvas, needles, cutters and most other supplies needed to complete the projects in this book are available at craft and needlework stores and through mail order catalogs. Other supplies are available at fabric, hardware and discount stores.

needles & other stitching tools

Blunt-end tapestry needles are used for stitching plastic canvas. Choose a No. 16 needle for stitching 5- and 7-count, a No. 18 for stitching 10-count and a No. 24 for stitching 14-count canvas. A small pair of embroidery scissors for snipping yarn is handy. Try using needle-nosed jewelry pliers for pulling the needle through several thicknesses of canvas and out of tight spots too small for your hand.

stitching the canvas

Stitching Instructions for each section are found after the Cutting Instructions. First, refer to the illustrations of basic stitches found on pages 156-157 to familiarize yourself with the stitches used. Illustrations will be found near the graphs for pieces worked using special stitches. Follow the numbers on the tiny graph beside the illustration to make each stitch – bring your needle up from the back of the work on odd numbers and down through 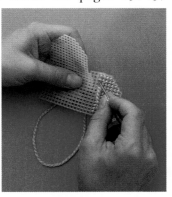 the front of the work on the even numbers.

Before beginning, read the Stitching Instructions to get an overview of what you'll be doing. You'll find that some pieces are stitched using colors and stitches indicated on graphs, and for other pieces you will be given a color and stitch to use to cover the entire piece.

Cut yarn lengths between 18" [45.7cm] to 36" [91.4cm]. Thread needle; do not tie a knot in the end. Bring your needle up through the canvas from the back, leaving a short length of yarn on the wrong side of the canvas. As you begin to stitch, work over this short length of yarn. If you are beginning with Continental Stitches, leave a 1" [2.5cm] length, but if you are working longer stitches, leave a longer length.

In order for graph colors to contrast well, graph colors may not match yarn colors. For instance, a light yellow may be selected to represent the metallic cord color gold, or a light blue may represent white yarn.

When following a graph showing several colors, you may want to work all the stitches of one color at the same time. Some stitchers prefer to work with several colors at once by threading each on a separate needle and letting the yarn not being used hang on the wrong side of the work. Either way, remember that strands of yarn run across the wrong side of the work may show through the stitches from the front.

As you stitch, try to maintain an even tension on the yarn. Loose stitches will look uneven, and tight stitches will let the canvas show through. If your yarn twists as you work, you may want to let your needle and yarn hang and untwist occasionally.

When you end a section of stitching or finish a thread, weave the yarn through the back side of your last few stitches, then trim it off.

construction & assembly

After all pieces of an item needing assembly are stitched, you will find the order of assembly is listed in the Stitching Instructions and sometimes illustrated in Diagrams found with the graphs. For best results, join pieces in the order written. Refer to the Stitch Key and to the directives near the graphs for precise attachments.

finishing tips

To combat glue strings when using a hot glue gun, practice a swirling motion as you work. After placing the drop of glue on your work, lift the gun slightly and swirl to break the stream of glue, as if you were making an ice cream cone. Have a cup of water handy when gluing. For those times that you'll need to touch the glue, first dip your finger into the water just enough to dampen it. This will minimize the glue sticking to your finger, and it will cool and set the glue more quickly.

To attach beads, use a bit more glue to form a cup around the bead. If too much shows after drying, use a craft knife to trim off excess glue.

Scotchguard® or other fabric protectors may be used on your finished projects. However, avoid using a permanent marker if you plan to use a fabric protector, and be sure to remove all other markings before stitching. Fabric protectors can cause markings to bleed, staining yarn.

for more information

Sometimes even the most experienced needlecrafters can find themselves having trouble following instructions. If you have difficulty completing your project, write to Plastic Canvas Editors, The Needlecraft Shop, 23 Old Pecan Road, Big Sandy, Texas 75755 (903) 636-4000 or (800) 259-4000, www.needlecraftshop.com.

stitch guide

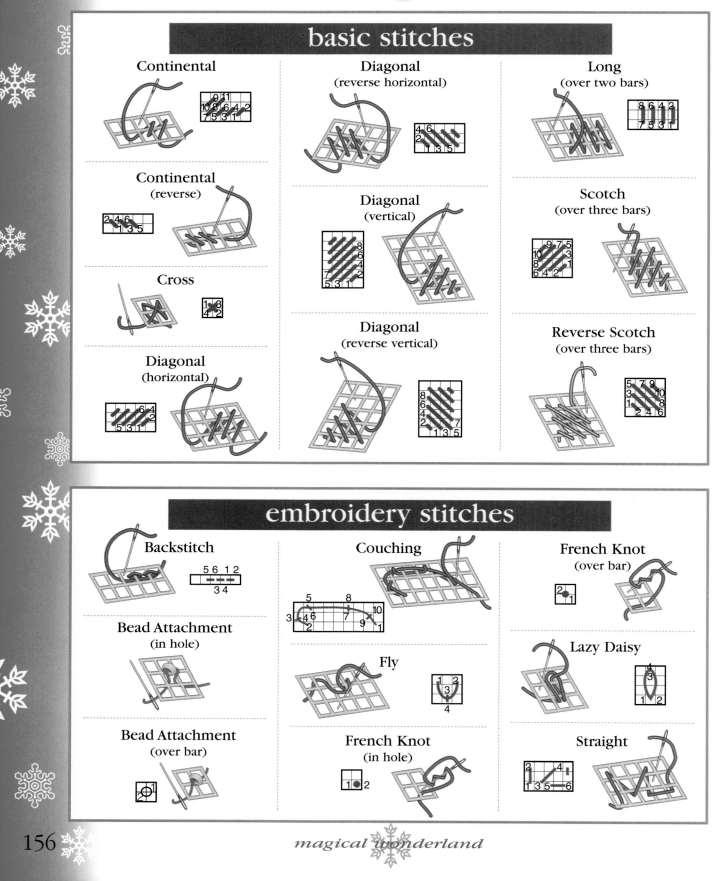

basic stitches

Continental

Continental (reverse)

Cross

Diagonal (horizontal)

Diagonal (reverse horizontal)

Diagonal (vertical)

Diagonal (reverse vertical)

Long (over two bars)

Scotch (over three bars)

Reverse Scotch (over three bars)

embroidery stitches

Backstitch

Bead Attachment (in hole)

Bead Attachment (over bar)

Couching

Fly

French Knot (in hole)

French Knot (over bar)

Lazy Daisy

Straight

magical wonderland

specialty stitches

Alternate Scotch
(over three bars)

Leaf

Smyrna Cross

Modified Turkey Work

Star Rhodes

Lark's Head Knot

Mosaic

Lark's Head Knot
(continuous)

Sheaf

---

finishing stitches

Herringbone Overcast

Overcast

Whipstitch

Herringbone Whipstitch

Overcast
(looped)

Whipstitch
(looped)

acknowledgments

We would like to express our appreciation to the many people who helped create this book. Our special thanks go to each of the talented designers who contributed original designs. We also wish to express our gratitude to the following manufacturers for their generous contribution of materials and supplies for some of the featured projects:

holy beginnings

Darice®: 10-mesh Plastic Canvas for Noel Wreath.

Uniek, Inc.: Needloft® Yarn for We Three Kings. Plastic Canvas and Metallic Cord for Beribboned Treasures.

DMC®: Pearl Cotton (coton pérle) for Noel Wreath. Six-strand Embroidery Floss for Snowman Manger.

Offray: Ribbon for Deluxe Gift Boxes.

Wrights®: Tassels for Deluxe Gift Boxes. Trims for Beribboned Treasures.

Kreinik: Tapestry™ Braid for Snowman Manger. Metallic Braid for Noel Wreath.

Westwater Enterprise: Gold Buttons for Beribboned Treasures.

snow friends

Darice®: 7-mesh Plastic Canvas for Merry Winter Carolers.

Uniek, Inc.: Needloft® Yarn for Merry Winter Carolers, Mr. & Mrs. Snowman.

DMC®: Pearl Cotton (coton pérle) and Six-strand Embroidery Floss for Merry Winter Carolers.

Coats & Clark: Worsted-weight Yarn for Mr. & Mrs. Snowman.

country charm

Darice®: 7-mesh Plastic Canvas for My First Pony, Birdhouse Gift Box, Joy To The World Christmas Stocking, Holiday Charmer, Winter Wonderland, Holiday Utensil Holder, Handy Helpers Winter Warmers.

Uniek, Inc.: Needloft® Yarn for My First Pony, Birdhouse Gift Box, Joy To The World Christmas Stocking, Holiday Charmer, Winter Wonderland.

DMC®: Pearl Cotton (coton pérle) for Joy To The World Christmas Stocking, Holiday Charmer, Winter Wonderland, Handy Helpers Winter Warmers. Six-strand Embroidery Floss for Gingerbread Treats.

Kreinik: Tapestry™ Braid for Gingerbead Treats.

Walnut Hollow: Bezel Clock Movement for My First Pony.

Coats & Clark: Red Heart Classic Yarn for Holiday Utensil Holder. Red Heart Super Saver Yarn for Handy Helps Winter Warmers

yuletide traditions

Darice®: 7-mesh Plastic Canvas for Christmas In Your Heart, Santa's Christmas Shoppe.

Uniek, Inc.: Needloft® Yarn for Christmas In Your Heart, Santa's Christmas Shoppe, Victorian Ornaments, Silverbells Place Mat. Metallic Cord For Silverbells Place Mat. Quick Shapes® for Tabletop Christmas Tree.

DMC®: Pearl Cotton (coton pérle) for Christmas In Your Heart, Santa's Christmas Shoppe. Six-strand Embroidery Floss for Birdseed Snowman, Santa's Christmas Shoppe, Victorian Ornaments.

Kreinik: Tapestry™ Braid for Birdseed Snowman. Metallic Ribbon for Christmas In Your Heart.

J&P Coats®/Coats & Clark: Yarn for Christmas In Your Heart, Tabletop Christmas Tree.

glimmer & glow

Darice®: 7-mesh Plastic Canvas for Holiday Table Runner, Santa's Candy Cane Holder, Jolly Candles. Wiggle Eyes for Jolly Candles. Acrylic Rhinestones for Jolly Candles.

Uniek, Inc.: 7-mesh Plastic Canvas for Arygyle Mug Insert & Coaster, Holly Holiday Frame. Needloft® Yarn for Arygle Mug Insert & Coaster, Holiday Table Runner, Holly Holiday Frame, Santa's Candy Cane Holder. Plastic Canvas and Metallic Cord for Beribboned Treasures.

DMC®: Pearl Cotton (coton pérle) for Santa's Candy Cane Holder. Six-strand Embroidery Floss for Mistletoe & Magic.

Crafters Pride: Plastic Snap-together Mug for Argyle Mug Insert & Coaster.

Rainbow Gallery: Metallic Yarn for Argyle Mug Insert & Coaster.

angel gathering

Darice®: 7-mesh Plastic Canvas for Angel Bell. 14-mesh Plastic Canvas for Angel Tree Topper.

Uniek, Inc.: 7-mesh Plastic Canvas for Herald Angels Organizer. Needloft Yarn for Angel Bell, Angelic Bath Set, Angels Over Bethlehem. Plastic Canvas and Metallic Cord for Beribboned Treasures.

DMC®: Pearl Cotton (coton pérle) for Angel Bell. Six-strand Embroidery Floss for Snow Angels, Angel Bell, Angel Tree Topper.

Mill Hill: Gay Bowles Sales, Inc., beads for Angel Bell.

Spinrite®: Bernat® Berella® "4"® Yarn for Herald Angels Organizer.

Kreinik: Tapestry™ Braid for Snow Angels. Metallic Ribbon for Herald Angels Organizer. Metallic Braid for Herald Angels Organizer, Angel Bell, Angel Tree Topper.

Beacon™: Fabri-Tac™ Glue for Angel Tree Topper.

pattern index

designer index